Penguin Books

YOU
CAN
BE
HAPPY

Amanda Gore is a physiotherapist with a major in psychology, and a master practitioner of neurolinguistics. A professional speaker and motivator, she is an expert on leadership, communication, relationships, lifestyle and stress. Over the past 20 years she has given her highly entertaining presentations – on topics such as how to lead and live 'out loud' – all over the world.

YOU CAN BE HAPPY

Amanda Gore

PENGUIN BOOKS

PENGUIN BOOKS

Published by the Penguin Group
Penguin Group (Australia)
250 Camberwell Road, Camberwell, Victoria 3124, Australia
(a division of Pearson Australia Group Pty Ltd)
Penguin Group (USA) Inc.
375 Hudson Street, New York, New York 10014, USA
Penguin Group (Canada)
10 Alcorn Avenue, Toronto, Ontario, Canada M4V 3B2
(a division of Pearson Penguin Canada Inc.)
Penguin Books Ltd
80 Strand, London WC2R 0RL, England
Penguin Ireland
25 St Stephen's Green, Dublin 2, Ireland
(a division of Penguin Books Ltd)
Penguin Books India Pvt Ltd
11, Community Centre, Panchsheel Park, New Delhi-110 017, India
Penguin Group (NZ)
Cnr Airborne and Rosedale Roads, Albany, Auckland, New Zealand
(a division of Pearson New Zealand Ltd)
Penguin Books (South Africa) (Pty) Ltd
24 Sturdee Avenue, Rosebank, Johannesburg 2196, South Africa

Penguin Books Ltd, Registered Offices: 80 Strand, London WC2R 0RL, England

5 7 9 10 8 6 4

Cover designed by Brad Maxwell © Penguin Group (Australia)
Text designed by Lynn Twelftree © Penguin Group (Australia)
Typeset in Sabon 10/13.5pt by Midland Typesetters, Maryborough, Victoria
Printed and bound in Australia by McPherson's Printing Group,
Maryborough, Victoria

National Library of Australia
Cataloguing-in-Publication data:

Gore, Amanda, 1954– .
You can be happy.

ISBN 0 14 300192 2.

1. Happiness. 2. Contentment. 3. Self-actualization
(Psychology). I. Title.

158.1

www.penguin.com.au

contents

acknowledgements

I would never have started writing these articles if Maree Curtis, an amazing editor, had not invited me to do so and then encouraged and supported me along the way – thanks, Maree.

My thanks also to my publisher, Jan Ogilvie, who approached me to put the articles together and form this book – and then helped me!

I'm sincerely grateful to my readers who have written to me with ideas. And to my mother, sister, brother, their families, and my friends, many of whom appear in this book either in person or via inspiration.

you can be happy –
all the time

There's an old story about a kitten that is running round and round in circles chasing its tail. A big old cat wanders up to the kitten and asks it, 'What are you doing?' The kitten breathlessly answers, 'Someone told me that happiness is in my tail so I'm trying to catch it!'

'That's funny,' says the wise old cat, 'I find that if I go about living my life, happiness just seems to follow me!'

How often have you heard a similar story with the same message? Actively searching for 'things' that will make us happy – expecting happiness to come when we have more money, a new car, a guitar, a bigger house, a better body, the perfect partner, more of anything, and thinking others or new places will bring us happiness – is about as useful as the kitten chasing its tail. Even if the kitten does catch its tail, it would bite it and then be unhappy with the pain!

For the cynical parts of us that are sneering at the idea of being happy all the time and at how trite this sounds, there are probably equal numbers of parts that want to believe we can be happy – almost all the time, anyway. Even in the midst of misery and crises, there can be happy moments.

Part of being happy is to accept that life is like a long river – it has many sections – tranquil pools hidden in rock corners, followed by smooth flowing streams winding through gentle fields, interspersed with white water churning over rocks in canyons, and then slow-moving, muddy, winding old delta basins – they are all components of the river.

Life will never be continuous, smooth, flowing water, although human nature wants it to be! And yet instead of accepting white water or rough patches as part of life's 'rich pageant', process and flow, we agonise, worry, become sad or depressed – we lose our perspective, we call ourselves 'unhappy'.

We forget to look at, or have a sense of, the river from above and to recognise this as just a rough section. There are more smooth streams to come. Without this balance of rough and smooth, the journey down the river of life would be very boring! We would never learn anything.

So there are periods when life is tough and there are challenging lessons to learn; we all go through these. Some people are at least content, if not delirious with joy, even during these times; they recognise the value of keeping the lessons and experiences of life in perspective, of being grateful for little and big things, of understanding that calm follows stormy waters and vice versa.

Some people choose to sit by the river bank in one spot – they watch this one section and that's their life. They are uninvolved and they watch others float by. For them, life is the same all the time – it's bland, boring and predictable.

Others jump right in at the head of the river and they experience everything the river has to offer. They whoop and yell and scream with the excitement of the white water and relax and recover in the lagoons, before they head out again.

Still others climb into a boat and sail their way down the river. They are involved as fully in the experience as the swimmers! The boat gives them a choice – they can jump into the water or climb out for a rest when necessary. They can actively participate in life or just go along for the ride, or both.

And then there are those who board a helicopter and soar above the water and see the whole picture – the boats, the observers, the swimmers, the rapids, the calm sections – all the aspects.

Daniel Goleman wrote a brilliant book called *Emotional Intelligence* which is a 'must read' for anyone interacting with other people – especially at work. He introduces the often ignored, but crucial, emotional aspects of the relating skills required for managing people. In his opinion, it's IQ that will make us successful candidates at interviews, but EQ that will make you an effective and popular manager and CEO material.

My mind started working overtime on this idea and I began to think that there might be a Happiness Intelligence (HQ) as well! What are people with high HQ like? They smile a lot; laugh often and out loud; they are in touch with their feelings and can easily express them; they are people who have the ability and skills to be optimistic; they do things they enjoy and enjoy things they do; they make an effort to maximise their physical health; they pay attention to mental, spiritual and emotional aspects of life; they feel connected with themselves and their friends; they are energy-givers and make others feel good just by their presence; they are grateful for all sorts of things; they have lots of friends and good relationships and understand the importance of these relationships; they have a good sense of humour; they recognise they are happy and they work to stay that way. In short, people with high HQ are happy most of the time, if not all of the time.

People with high HQ realise there is no 'big bang event' of happiness that, like a magic wand, will make them happy. They look for lots of small moments of happiness, and the more they find, the more often they are happy. Like a dotted line with smaller and smaller spaces until it's a solid line of happiness!

Naive as it sounds – especially to the cynics out there – I still think it is possible to feel happy all the time. But by 'happy', I don't mean jumping for joy and laughing every waking moment.

By 'happy all the time', I mean a sense of deep contentment we can feel about ourselves and our lives that can underlie everything we do; an understanding and a sense that things are as they are meant to be – an acceptance of what is. A sense that we can change and/or make a difference if we choose, and that as tough as times may be, there are still joyful moments if we look for them.

People with high HQ are those who can be in any or all of the river positions. They can be in the helicopter one day or minute, then plunge right into the cold water; then they may sit on the shore for a while, or rest in the boat in a tranquil pool; or brave the rapids in the boat; or just swim for exercise in the smooth flowing part.

They know that they do not have control of the river, but to some degree they can control where they are and what they are doing and what they are thinking about the river or that particular phase of their life. This knowing that they have choice is an important criteria for high HQ. And the ability to understand and accept that, at times, they must travel through the rough patches to reach the next, even more beautiful, peaceful oasis.

We all know the obvious – that happiness is an internal state. As Deepak Chopra said at a conference:

> Health is not just the absence of disease. It is a state of inner joyfulness.

Inner joyfulness is what people with high HQ cultivate. Most young children are born with high HQ. They find joy in the most simple of things; they laugh hundreds of times a day; they cuddle and hug; they really feel joy and sadness and frustration and impatience and fear and can cry as easily as they laugh; they play and explore, and are excited about mundane things. In short, they accept and immerse themselves in all the experiences the river of life offers.

This book is an attempt to help you find, or re-establish and maintain, the connection with your inner joyfulness. To nourish, develop and grow your HQ skills.

It's about simple techniques to change behaviour and improve communication skills, different ways to look at life, new ways to think about events and relationships, or changing the things you say to yourself about your life, so that you can change the way you feel. It is a collection of articles I have written around the central theme of wellness – a main component of happiness intelligence.

Read them at random or sequentially – much like your choice of where you want to be in the river. Think about what the ideas mean to you and discuss them with your friends and family – the articles are designed in part to encourage us to learn how to be better communicators.

But above all, enjoy them, enjoy the experience – some articles you'll love, others you'll feel are a waste of space, others will make you laugh and some may make you think and feel uncomfortable – just like life!

High HQ people will make sure they find some benefit, value, meaning or source of joy somewhere in this book.

Those who have lost some of their naturally high HQ may rediscover ways to view, to listen to and embrace the river of life from all its angles – the helicopters, the banks, the boats or just the sheer joy of diving in for the thrill of it.

What you go looking for is what you will find.

relationship
happiness

1

gender wars and how to avoid them

Hands up all those who don't believe men and women are different! And if you don't put your hand up, where have you been living? All that stuff about we're the same and ought to be handled in the same way is questionable! Of course we're equal and deserve the same human rights but we are vastly different creatures who look, think and feel in ways that are completely foreign to the opposite sex.

The paradigm-busting book that started the serious debate on the specific differences was *Brain Sex* by Anne Moir and David Jessel. This was the first book that accumulated all the scientific literature of the time and condensed it into a 228-page book identifying and discussing how the brains of men and women were differently 'wired'.

Some of the theories and research have subsequently been challenged but it still is a groundbreaking work. And it does provide explanations for many of the frustrating differences we experience on a daily basis.

Other researchers and authors who have written definitive tomes since then include Deborah Tannen, a greatly respected American linguist who wrote *You Just Don't Understand*; Suzette Haden Elgin, author of *Gender Speak*; and of course the fabulously popular (and easy to read) John Gray who wrote *Men are From Mars, Women are From Venus*. They are all excellent books to help improve our 'intersex' communication.

In my attempt to make a summary of the differences (so you

can live longer and stay stress-free) I have modified a diagram of the two brains that a friend sent me years ago. I am afraid the original author is unknown. You will notice the obvious structural changes that have emerged after the rigorous scientific, double-blind, crossover testing that I have conducted over the last two weeks! And my life. Please note that some of you may not have all the parts I have included and that your individual structure may have segments that are larger or smaller than the ones you see.

According to Moir and Jessel, all embryo brains start off wired as for a female, and at about six weeks into the pregnancy, there is an influx of hormones. If they are male hormones, the brain starts to transmogrify into a male-wired one. If female hormones come in, then the female wiring is defined. So hormones do play an incredible role.

Apparently the differences in behaviour are evident almost from birth, are more obvious as toddlers, and hit full swing as the hormones of adolescence kick in.

What are some of the specific wired differences? Firstly, women can multitrack. That is, they can do more than one thing at once. They can do two or three (or more) things at once – no problem. They can use several parts of their brains simultaneously. Flashy new testing techniques allow us to see glorious technicolour displays throughout the whole female brain when she is asked certain questions or thinks about something. The male wired brain has spectacular flashes in one spot, then another – in sequence. Apart from keeping researchers entertained and employed, what does this mean?

It means women can cook dinner, be on the phone organising a multimillion dollar deal, read something, watch the TV, *and* stop the children climbing over the pool fence. Simultaneously. And it means that when a man turns on the TV he goes deaf, because he's busy using his brain to watch the programme. Don't expect him to listen or talk as well. Even during the ads!

Now, before letters of complaint start pouring in, keep in

mind that I'm generalising! There are always exceptions to the rule and according to my interpretation of Moir and Jessel's work, if 10 was a perfectly female wired brain and 0 was a perfectly male wired brain, we can be anywhere on the scale. So relax, you probably aren't a male trapped in a female body or vice versa. (Although it is postulated that the vast majority of gay people are men and that the reason for this could be an abnormal influx of female hormones at six weeks, instead of male hormones, when the physical embryo is male. And vice versa.)

What other differences are there? Women are better at verbal skills than men. We make more noises to people around us as babies. Boys make noises too but they don't need a human! They'll gurgle at toys, mobiles, the cot and themselves.

Women communicate more, and often more effectively, and are able to link the feeling recognition centre and the speaking centre instantly so we know and can express what and how we feel.

When asked about feelings, men apparently have to search for, and find, the feeling centre, identify the feeling, then track back to the word centre to describe the feelings and speak. But John Gray says by then they have forgotten what they found in the feeling zone so they have to search back again! So speaking and thinking about feelings simultaneously for a male-wired brain is difficult.

This means men are often unaware of how they feel and they need to sit quietly to work it out and then put it into words. Women actually use talking as a way to discover how they feel. We keep talking and talking (and talking) until we've covered all the things that could be bothering us and we discover finally what it is that is making us feel the way we do! This gives men migraines – because they are busy trying to solve the problems we are stacking up in front of them!

And women speak more words. I don't know the exact figure but let's say women speak 24 000 words per day. Men speak about 12 000. When a man gets home, he's done. We have 12 000 to go! And this is the way we 'connect' and share (very important in a woman's world) and nurture relationships, which is the most important thing in a woman's life. We are hungry for detail from you when we ask, 'How was your day?' This is our chance to share our feelings and love with you. Men are desperate to be left alone when they arrive home after a long day because they have talked all day!

Women have better peripheral vision. This means they can not only register more than one thing at once, they can see much more widely than a man. We see better in the dark and have a better visual memory. Men seem to have better long-distance, focused vision in bright light. Maybe so they could be more effective when catching that pesky bison. Women have a good ability to notice detail. We can tell when something is out of place – by a millimetre! Often that noticing is labelled 'women's intuition'.

Not to mention hearing. Women are more sensitive to sounds like the baby crying in the middle of the night or the tap dripping. In a crowded room full of party noise, a woman can hear her husband or partner talking about her or another woman at 400 metres! Men, as you will see on the diagram, have a whole particle devoted to listening skills!

But they have an enormous problem-solving section. This is great for work and their own problems. Not good for women's stress levels where we really just want you to listen attentively, making appropriate noises and face movements as we speak! And of course, we women want to talk a man to death if he has a problem. And all he wants is to be left alone in peace to solve his own issue. Do not take this personally, ladies! This is normal for men. This is the main purpose of sheds and workbenches and, in some cases, the toilet.

But our spatial ability is not as well developed as a man's. Men are better at 3D models and doing things like map reading. Women usually don't know where north is – other than up! And this causes lots of pain and distress in the car when the female is navigating and the male is driving. We try really hard to catch the name of a street as the man drives by at the speed of light and then, when we finally have a glimpse of something we recognise, we have to turn the book around! It's impossible for most women to not have the actual street and the street in the directory going in the same direction. We often confuse left and right as well – we don't do this on purpose to annoy men. It's wiring! We're programmed that way. Fellas – to reduce stress, you drive and navigate and let us talk! This will help the relationship stay intact.

Here's a goodie! Men will remember better when the information has some relevance to them. Who said men were self-centred? They can't help themselves! But this is not an excuse.

Of course, I'm assuming that we all can develop whatever skills are not inherent in us. Women can learn map reading. Men can learn to listen and to remember things important to others. We can practise visual and speaking skills, and men can start noticing more and, by paying attention to detail, can develop women's intuition!

So what about environmental influences? Moir and Jessel believe that the environment only enhances the underlying differences laid down chemically. And I'm inclined to agree. Too many of my friends with children tell the same story about being committed to bringing up different sex children in exactly the same way, only to find boys longing for cars, trucks, guns and pow wow games, and girls hankering for dolls and tea sets.

Testosterone is a fact of life. Men have more of it. It makes them more aggressive, more competitive and more self-confident. And makes them think about sex three million times a day! Women have oestrogen and more oxytocin, a 'cuddling' hormone. We fantasise about closeness, affection and love.

We also have a martyr gene that is closely linked to a guilt gene. This means we do not take care of ourselves as well as we could – we need to be more 'wise selfish' so that when we do something pleasant for ourselves (without the children), we are not attacked by the guilt gene.

Men show love by protecting, providing and performing,

the male

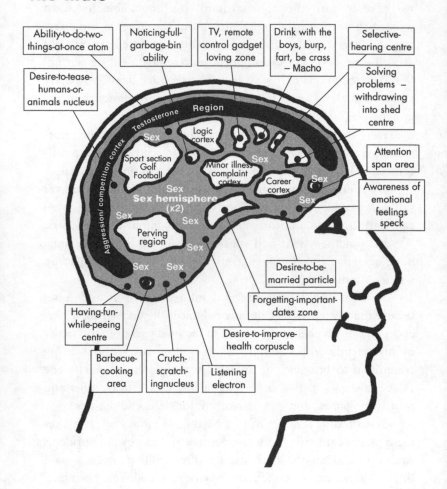

Ability-to-do-two-things-at-once atom

Noticing-full-garbage-bin ability

TV, remote control gadget loving zone

Drink with the boys, burp, fart, be crass – Macho

Selective-hearing centre

Desire-to-tease-humans-or-animals nucleus

Solving problems – withdrawing into shed centre

Testosterone Region

Aggression/competition cortex

Logic cortex

Sport section Golf Football

Minor illness complaint cortex

Career cortex

Sex hemisphere (x2)

Perving region

Attention span area

Awareness of emotional feelings speck

Having-fun-while-peeing centre

Desire-to-be-married particle

Forgetting-important-dates zone

Desire-to-improve-health corpuscle

Barbecue-cooking area

Crutch-scratchingnucleus

Listening electron

especially at work. Women want tenderness, caring, affection and thoughtfulness. And some sex. Women show love by caring, nurturing, mothering and talking or relating. Men want to be admired and respected. And they want lots of sex.

the female

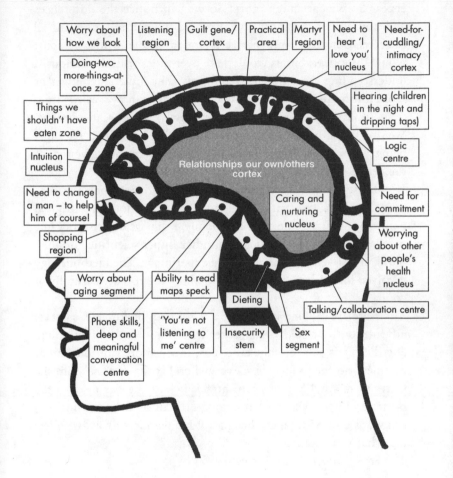

So what's the good news? Well, as we age, the differences origi-nally enhanced by hormones diminish as our hormone levels fall – so the strain of wanting a woman to be a 'good bloke' or trying to change a man into a female-thinking fella can be forgotten!

And why do we need to even explore this arena of differences? So we can laugh more! So we can notice the differences and honour them. I mean, what would women talk about if all their relationships were perfect? And a whole world of sport would disappear! Shops would take over the world. But seriously, understanding the differences and how they are created gives us more information, which allows us to deal with awkward situations (politically correct words for brawls) with greater insight. We don't take behaviours so personally. We can think, 'He's just being a bloke,' or, 'She's just being a woman.' In short, we reduce the desire to kill our partner!

These differences seem to extend into the animal world as well. We have two cats, Fox and Fluff. OK, not very original names but they're cute cats. Personally, I think cats are more like us than rats. So I conducted another super-scientific, double-blind, crossover, valid and reliable experiment. The methodology involved lots of lying about and watching them. Very carefully of course.

Here are my findings. He (Fox) is a real 'bloke'. He is brave, adventurous, intrepid, an explorer who is not afraid of anything. She (Fluff) is soft, cuddly, cute, coy, much more cautious, aloof at times and she follows him everywhere! If she can't see him she starts to miaow! She lets him attack her as she lies next to the heater and when she has had enough (because he hasn't noticed) she wops him with one of her paws! He wanders away, wondering what went wrong.

See . . . it must be chemical.

2

relationship day

Let's face it, Valentine's Day is here to stay. Yes, it's American in origin but it's rapidly becoming part of Australian culture as well. And yes, it's a commercial opportunity for most florists, gift shops, underwear manufacturers and card shops. But before you scowl at the notion and mutter, 'I'm not going to say "I love you" just because some money-making schmuck says I should; I'll say it when I'm ready,' think about this . . .

We are not taught about relationships at school; there are no school camps on loving people and how to have happy life-long relationships. The only clues we are given come from our parents and how they relate to each other, and to us. This is not always the best lesson. Although they do their best!

So as grown ups, why not use Valentine's Day to review our relating skills? In all areas. Call it Relationships Day if you prefer. It's a reminder in our increasingly frenetic lifestyles to stop and think about those we love. Whether it's a partner, children, parents, siblings or work mates – or even yourself.

It could be a time to explore your feelings about others and share those feelings. If that means a card or a small gift or a romantic evening, then do it – who cares if it's commercial! Who cares if someone else has reminded you to be caring – at least you are doing it. But only if you want to, of course; if you are only doing it to keep the peace, then you will at some level be discovered and the feeling you put in will be returned.

If you don't want to make it 14 February, then perhaps you

17

could find another day. One where you think about anyone special with whom you have a relationship – including yourself – and assess the current status of that relationship.

Have you told your parents you love them recently? Or how you feel about them – write them a letter and express any gratitude you may have, any respect or reasons for your caring. And post the letter. If the feelings are not so positive still write a letter, spew it all out on paper and then don't post it. You'll feel better and they'll never be hurt! As the saying goes, 'Don't fight with pigs; you get dirty and they love it!'

Is there anyone you need to forgive? Harbouring ill feelings and hostility is very damaging to our health – it can predispose us to heart disease and cancer. Work on yourself or seek help to find this forgiveness, which will allow you to move on emotionally.

How recently have you told your brothers and sisters how much you care for them? And why? How and when they have helped you and how much you appreciate this help?

What about your children? Have you been so busy guiding and disciplining them that you have forgotten to say 'I love you' recently? Or how proud you are of them and their achievements?

Friends are often neglected in this survey of relationships. We take them especially for granted. What about throwing a 'thank you for being great friends' party with little notes for each person indicating something special about them that you appreciate?

Perhaps it's your relationship with yourself that needs the most work. It's very difficult to relate well to others if you can't relate to your own feelings, needs and desires. Do you like yourself, respect who you are and what you do? Are you true to your values? Have you settled resentments from the past – old parental issues or sibling rivalries, adoptions, past divorces? Are you content with the way things are progressing in your life? In short, are you happy most of the time?

Does your relationship with a life partner need a review? Do you share enough; trust enough; communicate enough to be as close as you would like? Is there enough romance, excitement and spice? What are you willing to do if there is not? Are your expectations ruining a potentially great relationship? Are you too tired or stressed to be as loving as you would like or need to be? Do you have enough time together? Forget quality time – relationships need quantity time! Do you need to change the ways you relate to each other? Have you fallen into inappropriate patterns of reaction? Do you touch enough – non-sexually?

Take time out on and before Relationship Day (formerly Valentine's Day) to do R&D (research and development) and make a conscious effort to assess and improve your relationship. I believe we have forgotten this in our rush to succeed and make money. We make an effort for everything else – and continue to make an effort. We study, improve our skills, attend courses, network, show the flag, work late, and so on. We know we have to grow and develop in these work-related areas.

We usually make an effort in the early days of our relationships – until the 'prey is captured'! Then we relax and arrive home, exhausted, talked out, irritable, and collapse in a chair, thinking, 'Whew, at last I can relax , I don't have to make an effort.' Wrong!

Of course, we need time out to recharge our batteries, so take 30 minutes at the gym; or walk, sing, meditate, swim or have a sleep. Then remember that your partner and/or family are not there to be ignored, growled at or suffered! They will not stay if there is no effort put in to love them or share your life with them.

Find out what you need to do to enhance all your relationships and then make the effort to do it. You'll be amazed at the size of the return from a small effort.

Try having a partner Relationship Day once a month. Devote a day to doing something to enhance the way you relate to your partner in life. Something to increase romance, connection, intimacy and love. Sex often follows and is a by-product rather than an end result!

So welcome Valentine's Day – just change its name and do some R&D on yourself.

3

sex – are you normal?

Sex is the best 'relationship wellness indicator' I can think of. We all know that when the relationship is great, sex is great. We remember this when we are giving our friends advice or reading stories of couples in trouble.

When our own sex life is in trouble, we develop amnesia and forget that sex is a symptom and not the problem! We often choose not to notice or deal with issues that are slowly but surely eroding our intimacy, love, affection and caring for each other. We focus on the fact that everyone else, every other couple in the world is a) happier than we are, and b) having more sex than we are. It's the last bit that really gets to us.

Well, I have good news for those of you who think you're getting less than your fair share. In Rosie King's brilliant book *Good Loving, Great Sex* she quotes *Forum Magazine*. Apparently, four out of five people think that other people are having more sex than they do! In fact, a study in the *New England Journal of Medicine* by Frank, Anderson and Rubinstein found that one-third of married couples studied were having intercourse two or three times a month.

Another survey suggested that one-third of married couples went for long periods without sexual intercourse, with the average being once every eight weeks. And the bulk of these folks interviewed were under 38 years of age.

So, now that we've established the truth (that you are probably bonking far more than the average couple out there or that you are in line with the average couple), let's look at how to make sure that sex is always great.

Before you sigh and think 'not another article on sex telling us what we already know', I would like to expand the concept of sex.

For a change, I want to give men the benefit of the doubt! I know that most men (maybe with the exception of very young testosterone-pumping fellas) feel far more satisfaction from making love to a partner with whom they feel close and loving. The old 'wham, bam thank you ma'am' sex doesn't do much for most men's souls, contrary to popular opinion!

Just as many men as women are longing, in this era of uncertainty, change, speed, isolation and loneliness, to have intimacy, loving, closeness, sharing and companionship. The big difference is that for women, sex is a result of those feelings and for men (grossly generalising, of course) sex is the precursor to those feelings.

So there's the dilemma! Not to mention Rosie King's DD theory – desire discrepancy. In other words, when you want it more than your partner and vice versa. I love her practical, effective and compassionate approach to this problem. She says couples don't write off the relationship because they have different sleep needs, or if they like different foods or have different exercise patterns. Instead, they find creative ways to adapt. But libidos that aren't in perfect sync – well then, of course it's a sign of a mismatched couple! And instead of communicating and working out a sensible solution, it becomes a cold war.

When we are rational, rested and happy this is perfectly logical to us, if not obvious. When we are in the throes of a relationship in trouble, where we are both exhausted, communication has withered, touching is non-existent (except when 'he wants sex' or 'she knows she has to') and we have become 'married singles', we tend to focus on sex as the whole problem instead of all those other, often confronting and difficult-to-address issues.

Where do couples learn to communicate? Who teaches us the skills of emotional intelligence we need to sensitively and effectively let each other know how we are feeling? If you haven't attended courses or didn't see it at home as you were growing up, the answer is no one. It's the number one skill anyone needs for a great sex life! All great sex is in your brain anyway! (True, new research shows that stimulating the septal nucleus *in the brain* gives us an orgasm.)

A really satisfying sex life for most people is one that is an integral part of a loving relationship. In the courtship days, sex is fabulous because each partner is totally involved and frantically giving the other person everything they need.

He spends lots of time with her; he says beautiful things to her constantly; he tells her he loves her; he notices what she is wearing; he is romantic and plans weekends away and other surprises; he gives her flowers for no reason; he chooses to go out with her, not to the football; he watches little TV and then likes her programmes; he talks to her about his life, his past, his fears, hopes and dreams; he is a thoughtful and caring and sensitive lover, taking hours to tantalise, massage, tease and excite her; he remembers special dates; he rings her in the middle of the day to say he loves her – in short he is a wonderful, loving, emotional, caring, sensitive partner. He makes her feel like a princess, she is emotionally satisfied and as a result he is bonked senseless! He's ecstatic because he feels a hero and she can't get enough of him physically!

She, on the other hand, constantly gazes lovingly into his eyes; she sees him as the most special and wonderful man on earth; she considers herself very lucky and this shines out of every cell in her body while she is with him; she has that dreamy look on her face and that sweet smile every time she gazes lovingly at him; his every touch electrifies her as a result; she tells her friends how wonderful he is; she pays great attention to how she looks – waking up before him to make sure her mascara hasn't run and her hair is OK! She laughs at his jokes and genuinely thinks he's hysterically funny; she loves washing his clothes and taking care of him; she lets him eat anything and develops an interest in football just to be near him and share a common interest. She is always turned on by all the 'emotional foreplay'. In other words, she makes him feel like a God. Because she thinks he is one!

Then they get married, or move in together.

And the courtship behaviour continues for a while.

Slowly but surely, life kicks in. His focus shifts to creating a future for his partner rather than focusing on his partner. He doesn't understand the distinction and the impact that has on her and how she feels.

Her focus is on creating the perfect relationship and maintaining the same romance and excitement of their courtship. She starts to resent the behavioural change in him; his work is more important than she is; he notices her getting picky, wanting to 'change him', they both get tired and lose their emotional balance and very slowly they drift apart – emotionally and physically.

Lovemaking stops but sex goes on – the quality changes and this slowly undermines the quantity. Finally, the lack of it becomes the central focus and only then does the couple realise something might be wrong with the relationship and that sex is maybe the symptom of that. This applies to singles dating and couples cohabiting.

It's critical that we see the relationship as a separate living breathing organism. It has its own identity, needs and health status. And each individual in a couple needs to realise that there are times to do things for themselves, times to do things for the other person and times that they need to do things for the relationship even though they might prefer not to.

For example, having weekly dates (yes – weekly) where you discuss anything except children or work. Perhaps you could make these relationship wellness dates? Discuss how you are feeling about the relationship; what you would like out of it; where it is really fulfilling; your values; your visions of the future for your relationship. Create a safe place for you both to honestly ask for what you would like, what things you would like to change in the relationship, and so on.

Why not make a list of what 'sex' is for you? It's far more than just a bonk! Or what the difference is between sex and making love or loving? What is sensuous for you? What makes you feel sensuous? What touch turns you on? (Note for fellas: this is critical for women. The most common statement women make when criticising partners is 'he only ever touches me when he wants sex'. Women need ten non-sexual touches a day, minimum – and not all at the same time!) What makes a loving and sexy environment? What makes you feel uninhibited? What positions do you like best? What turns you on the most?

What makes you feel loved? What makes you feel loving? What are your most intimate moments together? What do you do that makes your partner feel special? What are your fantasies and dreams and ideas of romance? What's the most romantic moment of your life and why? What were the sexiest moments and why? Where are your erogenous zones? (Hint for men: women's erogenous zones are everywhere except her breasts and crutch – until she is begging you to touch them! Hint for women: his is almost solely his crutch – with the possible exception of ears!)

Take your focus off sex and forget about IT for a month at least and recreate the loving and romance and intimacy. Remember why you fell in love with them in the first place. Have they changed so much? Spend more time thinking about 'the relationship', not just yourself or how frigid, heartless or sex mad your partner is! Talk to each other – honestly and from your heart. Express your feelings. Hug a lot. (Just hug!) Laugh together. Be intimate, share secrets. Spend time together where you are relaxed and calm – create time and a space for your feelings to surface.

There is always the possibility of sex drive being affected by physiological issues like drug taking, medications or hormone imbalances, as well as by psychological issues like performance anxiety, depression, stress and exhaustion; but the vast majority of factors interfering with our sex life stem from a lack of relating skills and a breakdown in the relationship – and deep down we know it!

It's often easier to blame the other person than choose to

explore the unchartered territory of emotions, feelings and couple communication. And sometimes we need help, from outside experts like Dr Rosie or other qualified therapists or counsellors. This is a really smart step, not an admission of weakness or failure. Seeking expert help usually fast tracks the whole process and, with the right person, usually saves you months of frustration, despondency and struggle. And may prevent the 'roots' of your relationship dying.

Think of your relationship as an exotic plant; it needs careful nurturing, fertilising, watering and feeding. Ignore it and the flowers stop blooming; the leaves start to wither; the stems sag and your plant appears dead. But there might still be life in the root system – although it may not look promising. If treated well and nurtured carefully, the roots will support the regrowth. But if ignored for too long or nurtured too late, the root system dies (metaphorically speaking!) and there is no hope of recovery.

The fragile, exotic flowers are the sexual side of the relationship – it's a 'whole plant problem' indicator. How beautiful are your relationship flowers? What are you doing to make sure they are fabulous, colourful, numerous and healthy? What nurturing are you doing? What fertiliser are you applying? Take responsibility for yourself and make a commitment to change yourself and watch how the other person responds. Really try to listen to their needs, hear the feelings behind their words and respond to those feelings.

And remember, plants only thrive when they are regularly looked after. So do relationships (and therefore loving and sex). If you enter into a long-term relationship you are creating a garden of beautiful exotic plants. It will need regular weeding and watering and replanting and designing and gentle care. The returns are great joy, fulfilment and the satisfaction of creating a magnificent place of beauty, harmony and peace. (Where sex is great!)

4

love you the way you are

I was lucky enough to have my precious nephew stay with me for Christmas and it reminded me of how important it is to love someone just the way they are – and to let them know it.

Years ago when he and my beautiful niece were toddlers, I heard someone speak about the importance of telling loved ones, children in particular, how you love them just the way they are – and that you would never want to change them, they are perfect as they are.

One night I was putting them to bed and after reading a story I turned the lights off, kneeled down beside each one, put my lips against their cheeks and whispered, 'You are the most beautiful, wonderful, clever, funny, loving, perfect child I know. I adore you. I love you just the way you are – I would never change anything about you.'

Not only did they love it then, but as they realised it was to be a ritual, as soon as they knew the words were coming, they would smile, and hold their breath to hear every word. Five years later they still smile and hold their breath. I still do it now they are teenagers – they tolerate me!

It made me think about what we communicate to people we love. How often do we think, yet perhaps not say in the early phases of a relationship, 'They are perfect – I've never met anyone who has so many great qualities. I can't believe I've met someone who is everything I ever wanted.' That's usually the time we are most likely to say we love them the way they are. We certainly convey the message loud and clear at a non-verbal level. And it brings out the very best in us and others.

But as the relationship continues, we find out they are, after all, human! And there are things we wish were different. We love them but secretly harbour a desire to change them into what we thought they were when we first met them. Or what we think would be the perfect partner.

The message that they are not perfect, not everything we always wanted, that our initial feelings have changed, is conveyed powerfully non-verbally. This in turn can lead to changes in their behaviour and undercurrents of aggression, resentment, anger, fear, frustration or erosion of self-esteem.

What if we accepted intellectually that they are human (like we are!) as well as believing it in our hearts? What if we told them frequently that we loved them just as they are – and we wouldn't want them to change? They'd probably change! I'm sure many adults resist minor changes in behaviour just because another person wants us to change. As soon as we are accepted for who we are and loved for it, we willingly try to make the person who loves us happy.

Think about the people you love in your life; do you love them the way they are? Can you accept their foibles and idiosyncracies? If you can, let them know. Write them a note or say the words – and watch them glow. Ignore initial suspicion – if you have never made this effort before, they'll be wondering if you are drunk! And reinforce the message with repetition on a regular basis. If my niece and nephew lived with me, they would hear the same message every night just before they went to sleep so they could dream on it.

Perhaps as we repeat the words, we can remind ourselves that this person is worth loving for who they are and the way they are. And it will encourage us to be more accepting.

This is the way everyone wants to be loved. Maybe we could love ourselves the same way? We could tell ourselves that we love ourselves just the way we are – that we are perfect just as we are.

And when that little voice rises up and shouts, 'No, we're not! We need to change this and this and this; remember how stupid this was,' we can assess the ideas, discard the ridiculous, adopt the ones that are useful and still believe we are perfect – because we are doing the best we can.

We accept our friends the way they are. We don't ask them to change. If they need to change much for us to be friends we just don't see them again. We accept continual lateness as, 'Oh, that's just the way he/she is – they're always late,' or other behaviours in the same way. Yet if it's our partner, it drives us nuts! Although we knew it was a consistent behaviour before they became our partner.

To whom could you have given this message of love and acceptance? Have you lately? If not, send them a card telling them how you do love them – the way they are. And outline specifically some of the things you love about them – the message is even more powerful that way. Especially for your children. And send yourself a card. It's weird, but a good idea and great for your self-esteem!

5

how do we give love?

Have you ever wondered about how we show someone we love them and where we learned how to give love? There are no lessons on 'love giving' at school! And who ever asks us about how we would like to be loved?

With Valentine's Day there is a wild flurry of activity – sending flowers, doing things *we* think the other person would like (not usually asking them or finding out in previous conversations what they would really like); we surprise them and are loving (in our own way). And it may all be wasted! Well, perhaps not wasted – just not as appreciated as it could have been.

You see, the Bible saying 'do unto others as you would have them do unto you' does not always work when it comes to communication. Other people do not want you to do unto them what you would have done unto you. They want you to do unto them what *they* want you to do unto them!

When couples who have split up are interviewed separately afterwards, they often both maintain that they showered each other with love and affection – and the sad thing is that they probably did. But they showered with the love and affection that they would have liked to receive – not necessarily what the other person really wanted, or could interpret as loving.

And it's not as if it's a conscious thing. We learn how to give love from our parents, by watching them together and by our experiences with them. For example, my wonderful mother sends me a Valentine's Day card. In our family we have a tradition of demonstrative loving and affection and it's OK to say 'I love you.'

If you come from a family like this and start dating or partner with someone whose family is into handshakes after not seeing each other for five years, then the problems can begin.

Reflect for a minute about what happened last Valentine's Day, if you had one. Were you given love the way you wanted it to be given? In reality, you are probably thinking 'I've never thought about it' and possibly 'What a stupid question!' It's an important issue for you to think about yourself and a critical issue to discuss with someone you love, or are even interested in, or want to have interested in you!

One of the most important questions I think we can ask each other is, 'What do I do that makes you feel I love you?' and then listen very carefully and write down the answers. (Make sure you ask it in this exact way – it is easier to answer.) Discuss this article and the concept first because people need time to think about the answer. It's not your average, everyday conversation starter! Give yourselves a couple of days to reflect and then make it a dinner table discussion, or a Sunday sit down and talk-with-the-children type session. It would be wonderful to educate our children to think in this way.

You may be surprised at the answers you hear. Behaviours or words or actions that mean very little to you can be the thing that makes your partner feel loved, safe and secure. For women, it's often words or touch. Men are much more visual than women, generally speaking. So that may give you some hints.

For some people, it can be a spontaneous phone call to say 'I love you'; or recognising you are tired and arranging for someone to deliver a home-cooked meal; an unexpected bunch of flowers; a massage; holding hands; sleeping cuddled up; cards and notes hidden in unexpected places; wearing favourite clothes – anything that you do that makes them feel you love them.

What if you feel uncomfortable doing what they say indicates to them that you love them? Get used to it! How much more special is the gesture when they know you (initially) feel uncomfortable, yet you try to change your behaviour because it means something special for them.

In the early romantic days of new relationships, we display delight at anything the other person does. Whether it really makes us feel loved or not, we interpret it as loving anyway! As the relationship stabilises, our real self emerges and we may feel unloved even though our partner adores us. They just don't know how to let us know that.

As soon as you can, have this conversation with your partner and/or children and family. And have an annual update. Things may change or people may become more aware as time goes by of things you do that make them feel loved. Keep adding the new ideas to your list. Make it OK to say on an ongoing basis, 'What you just did then made me feel great, loved or safe.' Both of you need to make sure you put this new information to good use and practise the new behaviours until they come easily. Enjoy! This could be great fun!

6

are you compatible?

Remember a time when you fell or were (or are!) in love? You had found your perfect life partner: someone who was just like you, who laughed at the same things, thought you were constantly fascinating and had similar interests – in fact was your other 'half'.

Everything is rosy until a few weeks or months later, until the blinkers of infatuation, lust, love have worn off. We suddenly realise this person is not 'just like us'; is not identical; has different ideas, thoughts, habits and feelings, and doesn't always agree with us. Oh no!

Reality has hit us with a big thump! And we have to realise that the person we thought was our exact mirror is in fact an individual, from a different background, with different experiences and beliefs and opinions. Our real challenge starts when we notice and acknowledge these differences and ask ourselves, 'Can I live with this person, who is different from me?'

This is where compatibility kicks in. I added to my ideas by asking twenty couples what they thought were important aspects to know about each other to help assess compatibility.

You need to know yourself – to know what values, beliefs and behaviours are important to you in life. To know what you think about relationships and the sort of relationship you want to have. What attributes can you bring to a relationship? What would your strengths and weaknesses be?

What do you want in someone else? What behaviours and

beliefs do you think you would like in someone else?

Do you both have the same values about life? Values are the things that drive us, the benchmarks by which we assess things that happen to us in life or determine the ways we behave in life. How do you feel about trustworthiness, honesty, security, love, humour, learning, fun, integrity, fidelity, environmental awareness, balance in life? What other important issues need to be considered here?

How do your family backgrounds compare? Did you have similar socioeconomic backgrounds? Was your schooling similar? Were your parents happily married, miserably married or divorced? Do you have good relationships with brothers and sisters? How do or did your parents handle conflict? How do you handle conflict and how did you as a child? How did you behave as a child when you were angry – how about as an adult?

Does the family hug, talk about awkward issues, get on well?

How well do you get on with each other's family? What are your ideas on family and what makes a family unit?

How committed are you both to having a long-term relationship? Is it an important value? Are you willing to do what is necessary to preserve or enhance long-term relationships? What are your ideas on the number and raising of children? fidelity? religion?

Are you both optimistic or pessimistic? It's a challenge if you are generally optimistic and you live with a pessimist, or vice versa. It's OK in the beginning but becomes very wearing and destructive with time.

How do you both value time? Is one of you a human alarm clock and the other perpetually late? Although this may not be a problem initially (when everyone's making a huge effort), it can develop into a major source of conflict.

What makes you both laugh? How do you like to play, unwind and relax? Do you like to lie about and do nothing, or be wildly active and travel to twenty-four countries in five days? Do you prefer the beach or the mountains?

Can you and your partner laugh *at* yourselves – and *with* each other? People who take themselves seriously can be exhausting if you come from a lighter perspective on life.

What activities do you like? Are you both into outdoor pursuits or both bookworms? Do you love sport, learning, cinema, opera, music, horseraces – or hate them? And what hobbies do you both have – or would like to develop?

How do you both behave when you are tired, upset, anxious or stressed? What's the best way for you to calm down? What brings out the best and worst in you both?

And now for the BIG one! It would appear that the greatest predictor of whether a couple will survive the rigours of modern living is how well they deal with conflict. How well can you communicate with each other, especially under stress? How do you resolve differences? or fights? Are you able to agree to disagree? Can you talk together? And, more importantly, can you listen – really listen – to the other person? And hear the feelings behind their words?

What else do you think contributes to a couple being compatible? Perhaps it would be useful to use this article as a starting point for a discussion with each other or with your children. It's certainly not part of the school curriculum, but it might be useful if it were.

7

when what he says is not what she hears!

Over a very funny dinner a few nights ago, my friends and I explored yet another major male/female difference in thinking.

When a man is recently out of a relationship, whether it's a divorce or separation or the end of a long-term relationship, he is again single and begins dating. He meets a woman whose company he enjoys. He spends progressively more time with her.

The physical attraction becomes unbearable. He feels he needs to say to her that he is not ready for a long-term relationship; he tells her she is really special and he cares for her but it's too early for him to get 'involved'. They just need to be friends ('friends who bonk' is the unsaid message!).

He feels relieved that he has been so honest and up front with her. He thinks she understands the situation, how he feels, and accepts that if she keeps going out with him it is just a friendship with a physical component! She obviously feels the same way and is happy to just be 'bonking friends' as well. With no attachments, or commitment. Ha, ha!

What men don't understand is that women have a different language from men. When he says, 'I'm not ready to get involved with another woman yet,' she hears, 'It's too early for me to express my real feelings for you yet, but I am very attracted to you. I am wounded and hurting.' She thinks, 'I understand how he feels. I will be patient and supporting and loving and he will no doubt fall in love with me. I'm different and together we can ride this out.'

So, she continues with no pressure, and with great patience and understanding for his need to be alone (or so we think) or for time and 'space'; they have a great sex life ('how can he not secretly be in love with me?'); they have loads of fun and laugh a lot. Months go by. No hassles, no fights, no dramas. She is in love with him. She thinks about him every minute of the day. He enjoys her company as a part of the rest of his life. He thinks about her every couple of days or so. In the pub with his mates, or on the golf course, he wonders whether to go to a football game or whether to call her. He chooses the football game. She believes he is in love with her – no matter what he says.

He is stunned when six months later, after they have been reasonably constant companions, dating regularly and bonking lots, she starts talking about commitment! And she asks questions like, 'Where is this relationship going?' He reiterates his statements: 'But I said I wasn't ready for a long-term relationship. We agreed to just be friends.' She goes ballistic. He wonders what's wrong with her. He feels lucky he is not attached to this woman who obviously didn't listen.

He goes off and finds another woman who just 'enjoys his company' and really understands that he is 'not ready'!

Important note for men: most women (note I said most) do not, repeat, do not bonk anyone unless they are emotionally involved with them. Even more important – even if they are not too emotionally attached initially, as soon as the two of you begin a physical relationship (this means bonking) she will be emotionally attached. Men need to know this. Men need to worry about this and remember it.

Most men (note I said most!) find it possible to have an ongoing, regular bonking partner or partners without it necessarily being anything other than friendship. Sometimes not even that! They (not the men reading this article, of course) are perfectly capable of believing that because they were so up front and honest initially that the woman will be feeling the same way as they are – enjoying a regular bonking partner and part-time friend, with no plans for attachment, relationship or (freak!) marriage.

Don't get me wrong, fellas. I really applaud your honesty and admire you for recognising that you are indeed not ready for a full-on committed relationship yet. But don't expect a woman to hear the words! She will nod, look like she heard them; she may even repeat the words back to you exactly as you said them; she will say she understands and thinks you are wise to take this approach. Be warned.

She is often unaware that deep inside her she 'knows' he will change his mind as he gets to know her and spend time with her. Men need to know that when they make love to a woman, bonk, have sex, or develop a physical relationship – whatever words you prefer to use – she will become emotionally involved with you. (Keep breathing!)

Now you know this, you may be more alert to the dangers of a friendly fling after you have been open and honest and therefore respectful. If you want to keep this person as a friend for a long time and not hurt anyone, avoid sex with this person until you are sorted out. (Breathe!) This should dramatically speed up the sorting out process. Ha ha, just joking boys! About the speeding up process: not the basic concept! Think about it anyway, because I know men don't mean to be cruel, but that's what you will be accused of – leading her along, being heartless, selfish and a user – despite the fact that you were as honest as you could be.

Vive la différence!

8

words are easy

A million times we've heard that words are easy, yet we fall for the same old lines in relationships again and again. We allow people to say all the right things and do all the wrong things – or we don't notice they are saying one thing and doing another. Or we do it to others.

A man takes a woman out on a date after which there are a couple of common scenarios. One is that he has an OK time but doesn't think he wants to take her out again. He still says, 'I'll call you.' The woman (although she has waited her whole life for men to ring back when they said they would!) *still* waits to hear from him.

The other scenario that Dave Barry (the funniest American journalist) postulates is one where the man has a wonderful evening. He wants to ask her out again but is terrified that the next date would be more fun and would lead to more dates and so on until of course he couldn't live without her and he would have to marry her. So he says, 'I'll call you' and never does.

We need to look at the behaviour as the indicator of whether he (or she) will ring. In established relationships, how often do we hear what we *want* to hear, rather than what is really being said, or really hearing what is happening around us? Everyone else has a sense that our partner is having an affair – but we want to believe they are in love with us and faithful and happy in the relationship with us. We believe their words.

To change our behaviours is more difficult and requires

more soul searching and commitment. A friend of mine who recently split up with a woman he had dated for two years is a classic example of this. About to move in together, she decided against it because he said he loved her but he was having an affair with his work – which took priority over her.

He was so shocked after she called the relationship off that he went into 'what do I really want in life and what is really important to me' mode. He realised that what he said (which he really believed) and what he did had not been matching. The story has a happy ending because they are now together and there has never been a more attentive and caring man. But it did take a big shock for him to realise the difference.

How often have we heard, 'Do as I say, not as I do'? Children are far more astute than adults at a non-verbal level. They pick up non-verbal (which includes behavioural) messages very clearly, and if you are admonishing them for doing something and then doing the same thing yourself – that's what they'll do. If you smoke while telling children smoking is bad for you, they'll still smoke in most cases. If you tell them loving your family is all important and then you work every waking moment and never spend time with your family – what message are you really giving them?

I wonder if it would be useful to have a 'behaviour reflection hour' each week. To think about our own actions and those of others – and see if the behaviours match the words we and others say. Do your behaviours tell your partner and children that they are the number one people in your life? Or do they demonstrate that work is number one priority?

If you're single, do your actions say 'single but desperate' or 'single but active and happy with myself'? Do you ring friends when they need help or support – even when you really don't have time? Or do you just say 'let's do lunch' and ring in four months?

Our subconscious minds will always observe others' behaviour and at some level register that the words are not matching the behaviour. And that brings on suspicion, unhappiness and discontent. We may withdraw emotionally, argue more or change our own behaviour in a hundred ways – all for no apparent reason. We may not even understand what's going on. That's the time to become conscious of the behaviours of others around us. Maybe that will give us a clue to our feelings.

Think of the many situations in life where your behaviours and words may not match. Reflect on these and decide how you really feel and then make yourself congruent (meaning words and actions match). It makes life much more pleasant for us and those around us, and is less draining on our energy levels. Make a commitment to observe others' behaviour and base your decisions on what you see and experience and feel, rather than just what you hear.

9

everyone wants a wife

I received a wonderful letter in response to one of my previous columns from Mrs Doherty in Corinda, a suburb of Brisbane. This letter reinforced beliefs I have on the importance of the role of a housewife – and how unfortunate it is that many housewives are embarrassed to respond to the question, 'What do you do?' They frequently answer with, 'Oh, I'm *just* a housewife.'

Mrs Doherty has noticed the change in the way we live our lives these days – from a 'gentle world' in her youth, to one of fast food, rushing, urgency and chaos. A business career woman who had been very successful, she chose to make a new career based on her family, and she made some insightful comments on the value of a homemaker.

To quote: 'I'm one of the few females who admits to being truly happy. I work *at* home, rather than outside now, and make a comfortable, happy and secure 'support base', with clean sheets and towels, good food and wine, freshly ironed clothes – a place of security and peace from which my husband (yes, husband – not partner) can sally forth to confront the world. And I have all the time in the world now for me!

'When asked by various power-dressing, assertive career females, "And what do you do?" I love the look of bewilderment on their faces when I can answer truthfully, "Happily, whatever I like"! As someone said, I make life liveable while my husband makes a living.'

I want a wife like Mrs Doherty! In fact she and I agree that a major requirement for any person with a full-time career – regardless of sex – is a good wife. The trouble is, these days everyone wants a wife and no one wants to be one!

I'm here to shout from the tree tops the value of a 'wife' – male or female. Someone who does make life livable and cares for and loves us. Someone who delights in making the outside working person's burden and load easier to carry.

It seems that we have relegated the everyday aspects of living that need to be done for daily life to continue smoothly into a 'scorn box'. And one would never aspire to be a housewife or admit to enjoying ironing or cooking or cleaning because we are all so busy that the only way these extra duties get done is to use our pleasure, relaxation or unwind time. So we have cleaning people, gardeners, housekeepers, childminders, and all sorts of other help.

Which is great if it's really what you want. But I know huge numbers of women who clean the house *before* the cleaner comes so it's not too messy! Or who aren't really happy with the food that's prepared; or clean again after the cleaner because it's never good enough.

I say we should start a business called 'rent a wife' – or 'rent a mother'! Find someone who will come to your house every weekday; say a warm 'goodbye' when you leave; play with the children and keep them smiling and loved during the day; clean and wash and iron; make cookies; prepare dinner; and fill the house with wonderful smells of cooking food and inviting light, as they greet us with warmth, caring and love on our return from the career jungle. Or if you're single, do all of the above without looking after the children – more the 'rent a mother' model!

Perhaps it is an ideal solution for the rapidly growing aging population who feel there is no purpose to life now they are older and career-less. They could form lasting bonds with busy career people and regain self-esteem and confidence, knowing they are contributing in some way. Of course, many of these more mature adults might be horrified at this concept – they figure they've done the 'hard stuff' and the rest of their lives are for partying! Oh well, a few might be interested.

In the age where independence is God and we all strive to leave home and live on our own as quickly as possible, we might be losing sight of the importance of nourishment and support at home – for our wellness, career and general satisfaction with life. Granted, many dysfunctional families may never have had this supportive environment. I wonder if, in those households where both husband and wife work, it creates a situation which generates two adults too exhausted to put in the extra time to create this nurturing home life – for themselves or their children.

Even housewives want a wife! Being a housewife (or house-husband) is very often a thankless task – toiling away at all these unseen, unrecognised, seemingly insignificant details – yet it's these details that ensure the home works smoothly and supports the nurturing, closeness, growth and learning that creates family life. It's as though the role of a wife is the glue that holds the family unit together.

Many women would like to be able to stay at home and be that glue, but they can't afford it. Have we become too driven by the dollar? Could we be happy with a little less affluence, fewer possessions, a smaller house and a lot more love, energy and vitality?

So let's hear it for people who are happy to be homemakers – they do a fantastic job!

10

tv – the relationship destroyer

TV killed my marriage. This is a statement made to me several times over the years – mostly by women.

Every year or so, someone in America produces a study with horrifying statistics on how much time couples actually spend communicating with each other per week. It varies from five to 20 minutes. And it seems that TV-watching takes up the bulk of what would normally be 'talk time'.

Whatever happened to families or couples sitting around a dining table and talking as they ate? That process teaches children how to communicate, debate and discuss; provides opportunities to learn; and generally strengthens family bonds. Children learn most of what they know by watching you. Don't worry that they never listen to you – worry that they are always watching you!

How many people sit down in front of the 'telly' to eat dinner? This avoids the development of any communication skills, and destroys family units. Please think about how you and your family eat meals and keep the TV off at least until afterwards.

Or do you eat dinner in shifts? Teenagers rush in and out; tertiary students follow and then you, the exhausted last. Imagine what this does to your digestion. What about bringing back the old fashioned idea of family-together time over dinner every night or most nights of the week? OK, what about one night per week at least?

Lots of people ask me 'what would we talk about'? Try to avoid children, financial problems, mortgages and work! It's OK to cover those topics occasionally but aim to chat about other things like movies you have seen; feelings you have been experiencing; things you've read in books or in the paper; ideas for holidays or weekends away; 'homemade hypotheticals' (act out your own instead of watching the TV); the best things that happened to you last week; your achievements of the past week. There's a zillion things you can find to talk about – it just takes a little effort to be creative initially. There's a set of cards called the *Ungame* that provides hundreds of questions and topics that are suitable for families to stimulate conversation.

Another hazard associated with TV is slow whiplash – especially in men! It seems TV is better than any sleeping pill for men who use TV to unwind and relax. They have the ability to fall asleep within seconds of the TV being turned on. As they fall into deeper levels of sleep, their heads seem to flop backwards at unnatural angles. After a few years women stop waking the men for bed – they allow them to wake up at 3 am with excruciating pain in that strangely angled neck!

And just how do men who are asleep manage to spring awake when someone else changes channel via the remote control (carefully removed from the man's lap) and mutter those immortal words, 'I was watching that!'

What did we do before TV? I remember I was about seven years old when we had our first TV – it was roughly the size of a small container ship and only black and white. And I think there were two stations. Pre-TV we talked, went for walks, listened to the radio, discussed issues that we heard, read, sewed, worked around the house, visited people, went to bed earlier; Granny brushed my hair, and we did all sorts of activities that pulled us closer together. Then we had TV – so we could fight because Mum wanted us to do homework and we wanted to watch TV; and my brother and I could fight over who watched what. Poppa and the rest of us fought because we didn't want to watch *Pick a Box!* The whole family dynamics were disrupted.

These days people don't have just one TV. Often each person

has their own, so some of the squabbles over who watches what are unnecessary, but the isolation of individuals and the destruction of the family unit is even greater. We can all go to our separate rooms and watch what we want. With any luck, we'll make human contact passing each other as we go to the loo!

And what about the number of channels? Heaven help us when we have hundreds of channels like the States. Men and children would never speak again! And remote controls would be exploding from overuse all over the country. Not to mention the number of men who would develop RSI of the remote control finger!

Lots of people would never get anything done at all if it wasn't for the advertisements!

An issue I find really disturbing is what TV is doing to our attention spans. 'Channel surfing' is a 1990s term used to describe the technique used to change channels every nanosecond. TV programmes are designed to keep us constantly stimulated – something happens every couple of seconds to keep us interested, to catch our attention. The trouble is we unconsciously begin to expect life to be like that. So people begin to bore us if they talk for more than a few minutes without some bizarre behaviour equivalent to a nuclear explosion. People are developing the attention spans of gnats!

Horror above all horrors for me is what we are doing to our children with TV. It's now accepted that TV is a great way to learn at school and sometimes at home. But it's also a great way to shut kids up. And encourage bad posture, short attention spans, inability to communicate, dislike of exercise, nightmares, violence, diminished verbal skills and isolation. Boy, it's great for kids isn't it? About as good as having them play in the traffic.

I remember reading a study about an experiment in which families agreed to go without TV for some weeks. They actually went into withdrawal, exhibiting signs such as irritability, anger and depression – isn't that awful? How did we let a box with moving pictures start to rule our lives? To destroy communication in our families, and encourage all sorts of diseases? To isolate and disconnect us and help us avoid real life and living?

Please, think about how you control the use of the TV. Or does it control you?

11

single and happy

How many times do we subconsciously get the message in our society that to be 'normal' we need to be in a long-term relationship? If we are in our late thirties and have never been married, many people wonder what's wrong with us. Given the way people live their lives today, is this fair? I don't think so!

Other expectations on us make finding our 'perfect' mate much harder. We are expected to have successful careers. Women who choose a home career looking after children and family life are unusual – and obviously unfulfilled according to our stupid norms. They feel vaguely guilty that they are 'just housewives'.

We are expected to be gorgeous looking, to have great bodies, to be sensitive, caring, passionate, fun-filled, gregarious, intelligent, assertive and able to talk about our feelings; and to be great in bed. All this while we are stressed out of our minds! Women should be more like men and men should be more like women. We are meant to be able to communicate easily and effectively even though we are taught to talk, not to communicate!

Corporate life demands long hours and is often filled with job uncertainty and stress. We might travel a lot and have little time for our friends. Everyone is so busy that we catch up infrequently. Writing is too hard so we send a quick fax or e-mail. Dinner parties are less common – instead, 'Let's all meet at the restaurant.' We bring our mobile phones, so that when one rings in the restaurant, sixteen people lunge at the table or delve into their pockets or handbags. Family life is not revered and it seems OK, if not desirable, to make it a second priority. We don't understand the importance of personal relationships until later in life when it's often too late.

In a disposable society like ours, discarding difficult relationships is easier than working through the tough times and creating deeper love, intimacy, respect and understanding. We expect excitement and passion to be ever present in our relationships and are impatient during rough times; affairs are easier than persevering. We expect our partners to bring happiness and joy into our lives and to meet our every need – and we are disappointed when we finally realise they are human. Or, God forbid, that we are as well.

Contentment isn't a common word and is certainly not a goal for most. We expect a life-long, raging love affair that is constantly full of wonder, love, devotion and affection; and a partner who remains permanently fascinated with us and our every move. And we won't settle for anything less. Or if we think we have found it and enter the relationship expecting eternal bliss, we are badly disappointed and quickly move on. We don't expect to give up our fun, easy, single existence unless we find someone willing to be what we want. Not just how they are and loving them for what they are, as they are right now!

We are, on average, older when we marry and we are used to our independence. Compromise is more difficult and we don't like to give up that independence – to have someone with us most of the time, invading our space when we need it; or having to care for another when we are tired; or having someone who wants to play tennis when we want to watch TV. In fact, it's too hard living with someone unless they are exactly the same as we are.

So many people are choosing the option of being single and working on their own personal growth and development. Lots of people *are* single but happy. They would love to find a perfect partner but until then they'd rather be 'doing their own thing, not having to deal with another person's baggage'. And they are content. It is possible that we can be whole without being attached to another!

In fact, the best relationships develop when two single, 'whole', fulfilled people choose to be together because they like and love the other person – as much as they like and love themselves! They are not looking for someone else to make them whole or complete their lives or make their lives great.

So be single but happy and then find your life partner. Or just stay single but happy! It's OK. In fact, it's great!

12

men and the gadget gene

I have decided that men have a gadget gene. I know this because I have watched James Bond movies and I have conducted double-blind crossover studies on zillions of men and asked trillions of women.

The proof is in the number of remote controls men *have, play with and love;* and the way they can operate video recorders and program them. In fact the best person to program video machines or unjam a computer or do anything else that requires electrical sophistication is a 6–15-year-old boy!

Men don't just like to have one remote control: they like one for the TV; one for the video, the stereo, the microwave (no, of course you can't have a remote for the microwave but I wanted to see if the shops would be inundated with men looking for one after they read it here – it's part of my research!), the garage and possibly the washing machine (more research data).

And what about mobile phones? A woman with a mobile phone knows how to use it. She can dial the number and press send and end. And she knows there is a function key. She can see FNC and knows it does something, she's just not sure exactly what it does; and she's too busy to find out.

Men, on the other hand, love to spend hours fiddling with the things and reading the manual (afterwards) and working out every permutation and combination that is possible with this amazing function key. They store 500 numbers and can make it ring with the strangest sounds. They can also lock the machine very easily and when they ask a woman 'What's your lock code?' she has no idea what he is talking about. The man then takes four extra hours trying to unlock it – never actually admitting defeat.

What about watches? A man's watch is often a secret computer with hundreds of little buttons that make it an alarm clock, secret detonator, depth sounder, distance marker and compass – to name just a small number of the possible functions!

A female friend of mine was discussing her mate, who is so into gadgets that when a recipe says 'carve the turkey with an electric knife' he goes out and buys one! Another one says her man spends hours loitering in the supermarket in the 'boring' electrical aisles where there are batteries and electrical 'toys'. She keeps saying, 'We don't need these – why are we here?'

And think about computers. If there is anything worse than a man with a TV, it's a man with a computer. Men go completely deaf and dumb in front of that screen. One woman I know finally screamed, 'Why don't you paint the thing white and marry it!' Men (and small boys) will spend hours, days, years – lifetimes – playing with these stupid games, or working out how to do things that they will never need or use again.

And they get so excited about it! They want to show us everything – they don't notice that after 30 seconds our eyes glaze over and we start snoring. Even if they notice, it doesn't stop them – computers are like drugs. There are few female computer programmers because we usually become bored with such an intense focus on one thing for so long. Not that we couldn't do it, of course! If we wanted to.

The gadget gene is very useful in some cases when things are broken. Like faxes, printers, toasters, doorbells, taps. Some men just seem to have an innate ability to fix things – any sort of thing – as long as it goes 'ping'. Sometimes they don't actually fix it. In fact, sometimes they don't even come close to fixing it but they have a really good time! This starts in the early years with dismantling watches and other expensive items which, once they are put together, never work again. It seems the gadget gene is linked to the 'love of finding out how things work' gene.

OK. If you're still not convinced, think about pocket organisers. How many women do you know who have a pocket organiser? I know quite a few. But I don't know any men without one! And they spent hours initially finding out how it does all the things it does (like the phone). Later, it becomes a very expensive address book and an incredibly time-wasting device that takes him 20 minutes to find out what he is doing next week! And then some disaster happens to the batteries and all those dates, addresses and times are lost. Forever. That's if the organiser itself isn't lost.

There has been some comment from males who have read this piece that not all of them have a gadget gene. Maybe that's true. Could it be peer pressure or gender expectation that makes men feel they have to look knowledgeable and competent when it comes to mechanical or electrical activities? Is that why many of them stand around for ages contemplating the task before actually starting it? For those fellows who feel they missed out on the gadget gene department – stop worrying now. I bet you've got that gene that makes you say, 'It's all right, I know exactly what I'm doing,' so we all think you've got one anyway!

And perhaps some women have found themselves with this gene. I'm pretty good at working out mechanical and electrical complexities, but I am an amateur when compared with small boys. And it's very difficult for me to reset the time on the video or microwave following a power interruption, whereas the males in my life look at me with pity and scorn when I ask for help to do such a simple thing.

And I hate those 'do it yourself, any idiot can put this together in five seconds' kits you buy. I see what I want and I go to buy it, only to be given a cardboard box big enough to fit my car in. Then I drag it home and, once I've spent three days finding the screws, bolts, toggles, sprockets and things that hold my furniture together, I have to work out which bit fits into the other bits. It's all very confusing and frustrating. Women must have an 'unable to put a screw in straight' gene! Well, I do, anyway.

Although little girls and boys love to play with Lego (let's be honest, fight over Lego), not many little girls grow up to desperately desire Meccano sets. We fiddle for a little while and make simple, easy-to-assemble things but we baulk at building a nuclear power station roughly the size of a football field, whereas little boys will spend years doing this until their brother destroys the entire set. On purpose. Then they start on a submarine.

Perhaps the most telling factor is what men give their life partners for birthdays and Mother's Days. Black & Decker workbenches are not a woman's idea of heaven, guys! I know you are trying to be thoughtful and caring and it is what you would really love, but we don't have a gadget gene. We have an expensive jewellery gene!

13

a to z of relationships

There seems to be an A to Z of everything else – so why not relationships? Here we go . . . A is for feeling Alive so you add life to any relationship you are in. For being Amorous, Adoring and letting go of Anger. Think about how your father and mother reacted when they were angry and then look at your behaviour. Notice similarities? Admire each other and yourself.

B is for your Beliefs and Behaviours. What are your beliefs about relationships, and people of the opposite sex; about conflict and arguments; about money, fidelity, honesty, etc? All the things you need to understand about yourself that might be driving your Behaviour at a deep level. It's also for your Background – who you are and who the other person is. What made them who they are?

C: How do you Communicate? Clearly? Honestly? Do you listen more than you speak – or listen before you speak? Are you into Commitment? What are your feelings about commitment? Do you have Confidence in yourself and the other person? Are you their Champion? How do you handle Control? Is it an issue in your relationships? Be Compassionate with each other and love each other even when you don't like each other.

'Do unto others as you would have them do unto you' doesn't work in relationships. They want you to do unto them what they want you to do unto them! So ask, 'What do I do that makes you feel I love you?' Consider our relationships with dogs. We unconditionally accept our dogs as dogs – we don't look at them and scream, 'I wish you were a cat!' – so you can love your partner like you love your dog! And have regular Dates, even after you are married.

How much Energy and Enthusiasm do you have? They are important components of sex appeal. How Excited and Exciting are you and how much excitement do you put into your relationship? Does your Ego get in the way of love? How much Effort do you make to keep your partner interested in you – or have you become blasé and taken them for granted?

Be Friends First! Friendship keeps us in relationships far longer than lust. Learn about each other, ask millions of questions, spend lots of time together. Recognise your Fears and deal with them. Have Fun in a big way! And as much of the time as you can. The Fun Factor often flies out the window when financial pressures, children and mortgages take hold of our lives. Focus on the good in your life and relationship rather than wasting hours dwelling on the not so good.

Generosity and Goodwill will tide you through tough times. Give your partner the benefit of the doubt, and be generous with yourself – be generous with your spirit and your heart, not just your money. Grow together. As your life progresses, explore new dimensions, be adventurous and share new experiences.

Be Happy – in yourself and with life, and show others you are happy. Be Honest – with yourself and others and give the ones you love in your life lots of Hugs – it boosts everyone's immune system.

Intimacy is an integral part of a life-long partnership. Intimacy in many ways – not just physical. Make it safe for you and the other person to share your innermost secrets. Keep a part of you just for the other person so they feel special. Be Interesting – keep active and have an eventful life so you feel, and are, interesting company. Nothing is worse than someone who bores you silly at the end of a day. Live with Integrity – to yourself and others – and stick to your values.

J is for Joyful. Go through your day being joyful about life.

Even if it's not as perfect as you would like, you're still alive and the sun shines! Joint activities help keep you together – play sport together, learn to sail together. Do them!

Be Kind to each other and yourself. We often travel through our days being kind to complete strangers and when we arrive home we turn into monsters! Because now we can 'relax' and in the process we forget basic gentleness and kindness. Kiss and cuddle a lot!

Listen to each other – really listen, don't just wait for a gap in someone else's conversation to say what you want to say. Ask yourself 'What does this person really want from me?' and as Stephen Covey says, 'Listen with your eyes for feelings.' Laugh lots! Lighten up and don't take yourselves too seriously – life's too short! Love yourself and each other unconditionally. Keep Learning – it's part of the purpose of life. Learning helps you grow and develop; it keeps you interesting and interested; it fills you with wonder.

Magic Moments pass us by each day and we forget hundreds of them. Keep a book in which you write all those precious moments. In times of difficulty you can open it up and relive those moments and your body chemistry will change so you feel better. Have a Massage once a week to eliminate stress – massage each other as well. Make Memories! Create situations that will be special events in your life – they will become treasured memories of wonderful times.

Non-verbal communication is more powerful than you can imagine. Words account for seven per cent of the message being delivered to another. Be very careful of what you are thinking – or saying to yourself – when you speak because whatever you are thinking is being 'telegraphically transmitted' to the other person! You think you are hiding your thoughts that they are an idiot or at fault – but you're not. They know! Nurture yourself, your partner *and* the relationship – it needs special nurturing to keep it alive.

Be Optimistic. It makes you more fun to live with; it boosts your immune system; it reduces stress; and it generally makes life easier. Openness in your communication reduces misunderstandings and conflict. Have interests Outside your normal routine – hobbies, sport, history, archaeology, and so on.

Politeness is often forgotten once we are in a relationship. We are polite and delightful to complete strangers all day long and then we come home and become pigs. Play together – it's critical! Don't be too mature all the time – be silly and play sport or games (as in cards, charades, etc) as a family and notice the bonding. Where are your Priorities? Work or home? Do you have time for a relationship at the end of the day? Do your hobbies absorb all your spare time with none left for the relationship? Patience will help you travel a long way on the path of contentment – patience with yourself and others. Give each other Permission to be who you are and to live according to your values and beliefs.

Have Quantity time – not just quality time. Quality time is a euphemism for no time! All relationships need time when we just mooch around together. It's during these times that special, unexpected moments occur.

Respect and successful relationships go hand in hand. We must respect ourselves and our partner (and/or children). It's a basic human need. Find qualities that you respect in another – look for them and remember them in tough times. Where would we be without Romance? Make an effort to be romantic – it doesn't just happen. Plan for romantic weekends four times a year. Buy massage oils.

Stress causes more disruptions to our relationships than we realise. How do you handle stress? Are you allowing it to store up and kill you and your relationship? Do things to relax – daily and weekly. Make each other feel Special (not to mention yourself) in whatever way the other person likes to be made to feel special. Support each other and stand up for each other in public and in private – not many people realise how important this little act is for your bonding.

Be Thoughtful – do little things that let the other person know you are thinking about them. Make a quick phone call to say 'I love you'; give flowers; take out the garbage without being asked; if your partner looks tired, help them. I'm sure you have many ideas that will spring to mind. Be True to yourself – listen to your 'inner oracle' (that means the wise person inside your body!) and follow what it says.

Unconditionally accept each other. It's one of the BIG lessons in life – and it is very hard to really love and accept each other unconditionally. We can do it with our babies and toddlers and somewhere, somehow it disappears! Perhaps we can try looking at how we relate to our pets (especially dogs) and apply the same principles to our partner!

Value each other. Recognise the great things about each other as well as knowing your own Values. It's not easy to identify our values because no one really teaches us – we absorb most of them from our parents and they are such deep parts of us that we are often unaware of what they are. Be Vulnerable with each other – it allows real intimacy. Respect and treasure that vulnerability because it's a gift from the other person. They are saying, 'I love and trust you enough to expose my most vulnerable bits.'

Being 'wise selfish' is something that the Dalai Lama suggested we all practice. Whilst there are things we need to do for others – our partners, parents, children, friends – and some things we need to do for our relationship as an entity, there are also things we need to do for ourselves, to keep our energy levels up and to nourish ourselves so we can continue giving to others. Let the 'winds of heaven' dance between you, as Kahlil Gibran said in one of his poems – that is, be together without collapsing into the relationship and losing all sense of self. Andrew Matthews, author of *Being Happy*, reminds us to focus on the Widow's list, not the Wive's list. After someone dies or goes from our lives, we tend to remember only the good about them; but we focus on the other than good when they are around. Swap that process!

X: Bathe yourself in an eXcess of loving and happiness.

Youthful zest is attractive and engaging – we grow out of it as we mature and think we have to be more grown up! Stop it immediately – and grow down. Y is for You – you are the most important person to have happy, healthy and contented, because when you are all those things, it radiates out of you and casts a warm glow on others.

Zing, Zing, Zing – that's what our love-lives need more of! The Zest, the life, the excitement and all those things I have written about in the A to Z of relationships. Why not make up your own A to Z? See what you can come up with and make it a source of discussion in the family.

$$\frac{\text{stress}}{\textit{happiness}}$$

1

are you stressed?

The best place to start for busting stress is with ourselves. You are the only constant factor in your life. Everything else may change – your partners and jobs may change, your children grow up, your governments change, but you still 'hang in there'. How you hang in is a different matter!

If we clearly know the difference between our stressed selves and our relaxed, happy selves then at least we can identify warning signs that indicate a need for 'time out'.

The human body is designed to cope with crises – short-term stress. That's the old 'fight or flight' response most of us have heard of. When something physically causes us stress, like a sabre-toothed tiger jumping at us in the jungle or a car doing the same thing on a road, we automatically release adrenalin and other stress chemicals that prepare our minds, muscles and joints to catapult us to safety. This is great as long as we can react in some way physically so we can burn off the massive physiological (chemical) response to the actual event.

The twenty-first century is pretty free of external sabre-toothed tigers but full of non-physical stressors – internal sabre-toothed tigers – like worries about safety, money, job security, parents, children, relationships and so on. And it would be fine if the body understood the difference between a real and a vividly imagined or perceived experience. But it can't.

So, every time we are anxious or worried we release the same chemicals as we would if we were being attacked by a real tiger, although we can't react in the same physical way. It's not appropriate to run or shout or scream. It becomes internalised – literally stored in our bodies. Where it 'festers'.

And now for the bad news! New research is suggesting we become sensitised to stress. We might respond to stress as we do to an allergy, so that a stressful event from the past can magnify our reaction to a relatively minor stressful event in the future.

But wait – there's more! While we are full of these stress chemicals and our whole physiology is altered, our perception of stress is the same. So we know that what we are encountering may be a normal, everyday episode of stress, but the brain is signalling the body to respond far more than necessary, according to research by Michael Meaney, a psychologist from McGill University.

What does this mean? It means we really have to pay attention to our stress levels *before* they become a stress level! If we wait until we feel stressed, it's too late. So we need an army of quick stress-busters that will keep our stress chemicals at bay. And we need to know when to do them.

Unfortunately, we haven't evolved enough yet to handle long-term insidious stress without burning out. We are often unaware that our base chemical stress level has reached an all-time high. And has been there for five months. We are so used to it that we feel 'normal'. We have forgotten how creative, relaxed, friendly, patient and loving we used to be.

Our friends and family remember and remind us on a regular basis! (Which makes us even more irritable because they keep making unreasonable – to us anyway – demands.) They can act as stress barometers, and if we give them a code that they can use – a word, sign, symbol, song, note, something that lets us know they are noticing we are stressed – we can ask them what they see or hear that indicates to them we are under pressure. Give them permission to gently hint (or possibly scream) that you need time out.

But the best method is to be self-aware. To know our own

body and behavioural reactions to stress. What do we notice when we are (a) mildly stressed, (b) unhappy, (c) bordering on burn out, and for some (d) near death?

Firstly the physical indicators. Find a piece of paper and draw an outline of your body. Mark on this body what you notice, where you notice it, and when you are mildly uptight, tense or stressed. It may be neck or back or joint pain, or burning, tingling, tightness, stiffness, heaviness, dragging, discomfort or pulling. Your hair may fall out. Your digestion may be impaired or your appetite affected. Your vision may change. Your posture may slump. Headaches, heart palpitations or racing, sweaty palms, skin problems, nail biting, asthma, low grade sickness (flu, sinus, colds, etc), eye twitches, blank minds, a 'knot' in your stomach, constant fatigue, waking up tired after a good sleep, not sleeping well, and crying for no reason are all possible signs of stress.

Now, draw a similar diagram for your body's sensations when you are under a lot of pressure. What appears on the first diagram is what you believe to be the first warning signs your body gives you that you are stressed. It is in fact usually warning sign number 973! By the time you notice any one of these, there will have been 972 previous, milder versions. Numbers 1–50 are the ones to keep an eye, ear and nose out for!

This time, make a list of the thinking and behavioural things that will tell you that you are stressed. At a time like this, do you have a 'short fuse', or mood swings? Do you feel unhappy; angry; irrational; depressed; anxious; nervous; negative? Are you lacking in confidence; do you have low self-esteem? Are you irritable; procrastinating; snapping at people; losing your temper; uncreative; impatient; easily frustrated; taking longer to do simple tasks; unable to think clearly and/or completely drained? Has your memory gone? Are you grinding your teeth? tapping your fingers a lot?

What are you saying to yourself at this time? What are key or trigger words for you to become stressed? Is what you are saying to yourself the truth? in perspective? appropriate? Are you being kind to yourself with your words?

Become an 'inner travel agent' – be familiar with the differences between your mild, moderate and severe stress signs so you can accurately gauge your level. Keep your awareness of one or two indicators from each category high, and pay attention to them immediately you notice them. Develop a routine where you take stock every hour, or every time the phone rings, or when you sit in the car. Then take the appropriate steps to bring yourself back to balance.

How do you know when you are balanced? This is probably more important than knowing what happens when you are stressed. This gives you a target, a goal for which to strive. Ask your partner, children and friends to describe your behaviour when they thought you were really relaxed and happy. Find photographs of these times.

Then make a list of what you think you behaved like, looked like, thought like and felt at times when you were feeling relaxed, calm and unstressed. Put the photos and description up on a wall (or walls, or mirrors) to remind you of the base line. The best wall in the house for this may be the toilet! Where you see it every day – I hope.

2

we need to rest

I was listening to that cheerful (although slightly repetitive) song, 'Don't worry, be happy', as I was driving last week. Of course the traffic was awful and I was in a desperate rush and I found myself relaxing and humming 'don't hurry, be happy'!

What a great concept. Our near constant state of hurrying, combined with the 'urgency addiction' that Stephen Covey (author of *The Seven Habits of Highly Effective People*) believes has afflicted our society, often makes our lives a nightmare. A week flashes by and we breathlessly wonder where it went and what we did. We can't think of one minute of relaxing or going slowly, yet we have trouble working out what we actually achieved, or felt.

This is not wise. Our souls need time to catch up with our bodies. The physical speed at which we travel these days doesn't allow time for breathing, let alone time to 'smell the roses'! Or time with our children or partners or parents or friends. Do we really need to DO all the stuff we are so busy doing? Must we be actively engaged every minute with learning new things; or doing housework, gardening, sport, work activities?

Most people feel guilty or uncomfortable if they spend half an hour just sitting and contemplating; or listening to nature or music; or watching the world go by. And if they happen to realise that they are 'doing nothing' they rush to catch up on all the things they should be doing instead.

It's often during the 'doing nothing' times that our creativity springs back into action; or we solve a problem that has been bothering us; or we calm the 'troubled waters' of our spirit; or we renew our energy levels.

We rarely stop and genuinely celebrate our successes, or reflect on the progress we have made. We just keep driving ourselves to have more. More of what? Stress, urgency, sickness, frustration, anger, impatience, depression or just general anxiety.

I have always found that the more I rush, the more I drop things, spill food all over my new clothes, break nails/crockery/ glasses, lose papers, jam fingers, bruise bits of my body, knock over glasses full of liquid, leave my fly or buttons undone, fall over, lose my train of thought, forget important items and generally make a fool of myself! And the crushing blow is that I am usually later than if I had quietly and steadily cruised along.

Not to mention the irritation I feel when I am driving and I have skilfully passed 87 cars, changed lanes 140 times, sworn at 50 red lights, narrowly missed killing several pedestrians, only to stop at a red light and see one of the slow driving, no – crawling – idiots that I had passed fifteen minutes ago pull up beside me. Pointing out that all my cunning, bravery and skill had achieved nothing except the near death of twenty innocent pedestrians and the rapid destruction of my car!

A few weeks ago I was in Fraser Island with a conference and I found myself at Eli Creek. This is a gorgeous crystal clear freshwater creek that runs into the incredible 75-mile-long beach of fine, white sand. It's nestled in lush, tropical greenery that is filled with all sorts of birds and cute animals.

As I was charging up the walkway to the start of the creek into which I was to plunge and then drift back to the awaiting bus, I suddenly realised that I was not in a race. There was no prize for breaking the world record of getting to the top of Eli Creek! And that with my head and eyes down concentrating on my destination, I was missing the spectacular scenery around me. So I stopped, took a breath and started looking around me and enjoying the journey on route to my destination.

How many times does that happen in life? Our urgency addiction and our 'speed habit' (and I don't mean the chemical kind) destroy our appreciation of the beauty and wonder of the world around us.

We think that by going faster, achieving more, doing more, we will automatically find happiness. All this rushing is destroying our inner peace and making us sick. We need to relax. We need to rest.

So slow down. On purpose. Create time to sit and do nothing daily – or at least weekly. And leave guilt behind at that time – in fact remind yourself that you are taking a wellness approach to life and actively recharging your batteries before they are so drained they can no longer be recharged. You deserve this time – remember you're a human *being*, not a human *doing*.

3

10 commandments for reducing stress

1. Thou shalt not be perfect or even try to be.
We sometimes impose unrealistic expectations on ourselves. We think we should never be tired or grumpy, make mistakes, react rather than respond, etc. Be gentle on yourself – we usually expect far more from ourselves than anyone else would ever dream of expecting!

2. Thou shalt not try to be all things to all people.
Save some time for yourself! We all need a little 'space' to just breathe, be, stop and take stock. If we rush around ignoring our own needs and trying to satisfy everyone else's needs we burn out. And that's not good for anyone, especially ourselves.

3. Thou shalt always leave things undone that ought to be done.
When we are stretched to our limits and trying to do everything that needs to be done and more, the toll on our own bodies is severe. We usually attack our own immune systems. Unfortunately, it's not like we have a fuel gauge that says, 'Warning! Immune system on reserve!' so we can stop and refuel. We don't even know it's happening, until we become ill, for no apparent reason. Sometimes it's really smart to stop, take a break, relax, regroup and refresh before you go on to finish 'what ought to be done'.

4. Thou shalt not spread thyself too thin.
Taking on too much, working too long, volunteering for extra

work or activities, parenting, studying and working, travelling – all the things that make up life in the laser track (or today's society) – mean that we are all just doing too much to be well. Pace yourself and . . .

5. Thou shalt learn to say 'No!'

You can do this very gently and respectfully. It is respectful to yourself when you recognise your need for 'time out' and give it to yourself. It may feel uncomfortable initially, especially if you have created an image for yourself where others think, 'We can always rely on good old . . .' to help out.

For your sanity and energy and vitality, learn to say 'No!' Even if you say, 'Yes, but not yet' as a start. Remember you are a very worthwhile person and deserve time to yourself. And it is quite possible to say 'No' with respect. Sometimes, when you say 'No' you may increase others' respect for your time, energy and efforts.

6. Thou shalt schedule time for thyself and for thy supportive network.

Your social support – family and friends – are critical for a strong immune system. People who are isolated from family and friends or who feel alone become ill more often that those with even one or two friends around them. If you are someone who has no friends or family near you, join community or church or volunteer groups. Visit orphanages or old people's homes. Adopt a grandparent or a family. Join clubs, play team sports, go to classes and learn a new skill. If you do have family and friends around you, make time for them – they are very important to your wellness and longevity.

7. Thou shalt switch off and do nothing regularly!

I know, I know, you don't have time to sit and do nothing. So then you must plan time later to be sick! If you make time to sit and do nothing sometimes, you rest your body, spirit and soul. Now, I'm not being religious here – it's just that we all have a spirit inside us. It's the thing that is the essence of you, that gives you energy, zest for life, enthusiasm. It makes life fun and even childish sometimes. Most of us are so busy running around doing things we have ignored our spirit for years. It's still there – just very tiny and faint.

Give your body, your mind and your spirit time to regenerate, repair and revitalise. Busy disease affects most people in our society. It may be work busy, children busy, or just busy. If you keep yourself frantically busy all day every day then (a) the quality of everything you do will suffer, (b) you'll never have time to plan your life, and (c) you'll go nuts.

8. Thou shalt be boring, untidy, inelegant and unattractive at times.
Who cares what other people think? Of course there are times when we must be aware of appropriate behaviour in certain situations. But it's important to give yourself permission to be you! People like you, not your clothes. Wear Ugg boots and fluffy slippers; they keep you warm, they don't change your personality!

9. Thou shalt not even feel guilty!
This is a humdinger commandment! We 'should' or 'shouldn't' ourselves too much. We berate and blame ourselves and feel bad or guilty for no good reason other than we *should* have known (being mind readers) or we *shouldn't* have been tired and crabby. The next time you are feeling guilty, stop and ask yourself, 'What have I done?' and, 'Who said I shouldn't have done it?' If you didn't consciously set out to hurt someone else, then forgive yourself for making a mistake. Mistakes are learning opportunities, not failures. What do you say to yourself about mistakes?

10. Especially thou shalt not be thine own worst enemy, but be thy best friend.
If you aren't your own best friend, who is? Who criticises you more than anyone else? Your self-esteem is in part determined by

what you say to yourself about yourself, as well as what others say and think. Listen to the way you talk to yourself and be gentle, kind and loving. Be a loving parent to yourself and accept yourself for the worthwhile person you are – warts and all.

Reproduced with kind permission of author, Hilary Langford of Oliver & Langford (organisational change consultants), Chillingham, NSW. Email mentor@hilary.com.au.

4

happiness according to Dennis Prager

This month I presented at a conference in America and was inspired by a man called Dennis Prager. A well-known media personality, he has had his own radio programme for many years and is known for his insightful and profound philosophies on life.

At the time, he was releasing a new book called *Happiness is a Serious Problem*, and he gave us a snapshot during his presentation. In his list of eight barriers to happiness, the two that made me think the most were, one, the fact that we compare ourselves with others and, two, having expectations.

Nothing new here, you might be muttering to yourself – we all know that! But listen to the way he made it real and relevant. Imagine this scenario: couples A and B have a dinner arrangement for the evening. On the way to the restaurant, each couple argues heatedly after a busy and tiring week. They storm into the restaurant, hating each other but as soon as they see their friends they pretend all is well. Life is great. They may even call each other loving names and be very caring towards each other during the meal.

After a pleasant dinner, both couples return to their respective cars in silence, the anger and hurt still predominant; only now it's made worse by each one thinking, 'They are so happy – why can't we be like that?' So one of the two says, 'Did you see how happy John and Sarah are? Why can't we be like that?' And World War III erupts!

As Dennis says, we compare ourselves with people we think

are happy. The truth is often very different; the more we get to know others the more we realise they are not the 'ideal, incredibly happy' couple or person, in the perfect situation we had imagined. Beware what you assume about others!

This only goes to reinforce age old wisdom your grandmother probably told you – 'comparisons are odious'. So stop them! When you find yourself comparing yourself with others, stop and ask yourself, 'How well do I really know this person/couple/situation? Do I know the truth?' And if you don't, change what you are saying to yourself. Be more realistic; if you don't live in their house, you probably don't really know what goes on.

Let other people be, and pay attention to improving your own life if it needs it. Be honest with yourself and in relationships; be honest with each other and with your close friends. That's what makes them close friends – you can be honest. If you had a fight on the way to the restaurant, laugh about it with your friends, who will probably tell you they did too!

The other big obstacle to happiness in Dennis's opinion was having expectations. He linked this to the real secret of happiness, which is gratitude. I think he's right when he says if we do not have gratitude, it's impossible to be happy, and what undermines gratitude is expectations.

I have tested his theory and I reckon it works. Wake up and have a ritual of immediately finding two things for which to be grateful. The fact that you woke up is a good number one! That you are relatively healthy; you have a job; you have people who love you or like you; you live in Australia; you can laugh and speak and sing and dance if you want to; you have food to eat – these are just a few ideas to trigger your thinking. Then be grateful for sunshine; for clean air; for the beauty in nature all around you; for social support; for the ability to breathe – find something.

There are many things all of us can appreciate. Look around you and every day internally (or to others) express those feelings. Around the dinner table every night, make it a ritual to search for things that happened during the day for which you might be grateful.

Make it a habit to be grateful for something as soon as you wake up; each lunchtime and before you go to bed. I know it sounds a little over the top but it's very effective. Keep a journal and fill it in each night before you sleep. I resolved to do this after I heard Dennis Prager and it's great! As an extra technique, anytime I feel a little stressed, tense, upset or other than happy, I look around and find some wonderful things I can appreciate and I think how blessed I am – it's amazing how it changes one's mood!

5

stress-busters

Stress is a fact of life, but it doesn't have to be a way of life. And it seems stress is here to stay – in a big way! People are expected to do more, with less, in less time.

We are in the age of materialism with the 'nightmare of the two career couple', where both partners are working, and bringing up children. More single parents exist than ever before. Change and chaos is constantly swirling around us – at work, at home and in society. Cities are bigger, faster and more unsafe. We have more possessions than we have ever had before – yet there is more unhappiness and emptiness than ever before.

There is an old story bandied about in management circles about two frogs. One is put into a saucepan of boiling water – guess what happens? Not surprisingly, it jumps out. Very quickly. Smart frog! The other frog is put into a saucepan of cold water which is put over low heat. The heat is gradually turned up to the point where the water boils. The frog doesn't notice the subtle and small changes and allows itself to be boiled to death. That's not a happy story, but it does demonstrate that sudden change may have advantages. It's a different way of thinking about the change occurring around us. We can be upset by it or we can see it in a different light.

Life is really not about reality. It's about our *perception* of what's happening around us and to us – what we say to ourselves about it. That's the beauty of the human brain – we have choices. We have options in terms of how to behave or respond or think in the face of stressful situations. Between now and next week, think about how you think about the stressful situations that occur. And then compare the reality with your perception. Ask others for their objective opinion.

The meaning of the word 'stress' has changed in the last 20 years. It has become synonymous with distress. Years ago, it was generally accepted that we all needed some 'stress' to function well. What they really meant was stimulation. Without any stimulation – for example, if we are put in a white room, with no sound, movement, colour or change in lights – we go nuts! Being bored can produce a similar physiological response, or chemical change in the body, to being very tense. So we all need some stimulation, some interests in life to keep us at our peak.

There is little chance of people dying of lack of stimulation or boredom these days. It's more likely that most of us are lacking in energy and vitality, feeling overwhelmed, constantly exhausted, and having massive sense-of-humour failures! I think it's called Burn Out – the big BO!

The best way to avoid the big BO is to have a balanced lifestyle – exercise regularly, eat well, sleep at least seven hours a day, laugh a lot, meditate, do yoga, see friends, enjoy our work, have regular holidays, be grateful for what we have and have great relationships that support us.

Most people would have to be brain dead not to know the importance of exercise, meditation and the other aspects I mentioned. Yet few people regularly do these activities – because, of course, they have no time!

Not only is it the 'age of materialism', it's also the 'age of the quick fix' – what can I do that takes four seconds and makes me feel great? Firstly, remember that to really allow ourselves to recover from twenty-first century life, we need to pay attention to all aspects of our lifestyle. And make long-term (and often dramatic) changes.

But for those moments where stress 'catches' us unaware, there are some ideas that provide effective and quick strategies for busy people. Although the ideas may seem simple (and many of them are) they are not always easy to do when we most need to do them. That's where the skill lies – in recognising we are stressed and then making time to do something to bring our body back to balance.

The problem is we can fool our minds, but we can't fool our bodies. Our bodies store stress. We travel along in life thinking we are fine, handling everything, managing work and life. In fact, while we are combining long working hours and a frantically busy home life, we often manage to avoid sickness.

Until we go on holidays! It would appear that high stress levels keep our adrenalin and cortisol (stress hormones) levels high, which reduces the effectiveness of our immune systems. The adrenalin and cortisol, although useful in short-term physical stressful situations, have quite damaging long-term effects. Our bodyminds (we don't have a separate mind and body – they are intricately linked) know that on holidays we have 'time to get sick'. It's almost like we 'save up' to get sick on holidays. And we recover just in time for work again!

If sickness as soon as we go on holidays is a pattern in our life, it is a classic sign that we are not handling stress well enough along the way and we need to do something about it.

Begin to regularly practise stress-busting activities and different ways of thinking and before you know it, life will flow a little more easily; fewer things will bother you, people will say you are looking well and relaxed, and you'll laugh more. This probably means you are handling stress better. Your friends may wonder whether you have had a personality transplant!

Remember, these ideas are just an aid. As they say on TV, if the symptoms persist, please see your doctor. If we are swamped, overwhelmed, burnt out, often the quickest path to recovery is to see a doctor, or qualified therapist. If you decide to seek help (which is a smart way of dealing with these issues as opposed to sitting at home 'stewing with anxiety', analysing yourself to death or turning into a workaholic to avoid thinking about problems), remember that if one person doesn't work well with you, or suit your style, or if you don't feel comfortable, find another qualified person with whom you feel you will progress.

It's like flossing your teeth – as a preventive strategy we need to do it every day. We need regular 'mental flossing' as well.

6

a super stress-buster

At last, the cheapest, most effective 'stress-busters' I know: breathing and escaping!

Suffering from stress is a bit like drowning. The first thing it affects is our breathing. Our brain becomes starved of oxygen, which stops us thinking resourcefully in tough or difficult situations; our chest feels tight and we feel fear.

When in difficulty, the first thing to do is to get our head above water and take some deep breaths. That's exactly what we need to do with stressful situations.

Notice what happens to your breathing next time you feel anxious or tense – you'll find your breathing is shallow, irregular and only at the top of your lungs. This could be called tense breathing as it triggers tense behaviour. And certainly stops all sensible brain activity, let alone resourceful behaviour!

Do you remember sitting down to an exam? It's perusal time and you are looking down the list of questions: the first four are fine, but the fifth question is one you did not study for. *Oh no*! Immediately you would have stopped breathing! (Not literally, because you would die; but your breathing became very shallow and high. As a result, your brain stopped.) That's what happens in real life when we encounter a situation we perceive as stressful.

Here's the antidote. Take a deep breath, right down to the base of your lungs, put your hands at the bottom of your ribs and feel your diaphragm and stomach expand as you breathe in, then let the air out fully. Pause for a second or two and then take another deep breath. It doesn't have to be a huge volume breath, but it needs to be down at the base of your lungs. Your shoulders should be relaxed and not surging towards the ceiling! This is relaxed, resourceful breathing and if you watch someone sleeping peacefully you will see what relaxed breathing is like.

Every time you hear or read the word 'stress' from now on, or are aware that you feel stressed, consciously take two deep breaths. Breathe in, pause, and breathe out. It's the second breath that has the physiological impact, so it's the most important one. No one else notices, it makes you feel good and eventually becomes an automatic response to stress (breathe twice!) instead of the shallow breathing that puts you into panic mode.

Many people smoke under pressure because when smoking they take deep, long breaths – the same strategy works much better if you do it without the cigarette!

Although it sounds simple, it's not always easy to remember to breathe – but it is the single greatest weapon humans have against stress-causing situations, real or imagined. Stick a note that says RTB (Remember To Breathe!) on your bathroom mirror, in front of your desk, or in your car.

Another strategy in a world full of real or imagined sabre-toothed tigers is to create our own safe haven: a place where we can unwind, be ourselves, feel safe, be loved and loving, be peaceful and recharge our batteries.

This strategy of creating physical stress-free zones is very effective. To create a physical safe area, we need to find and keep a separate spot or space from where we live.

When we walk in the door, where do we leave our briefcases or other work-linked items? Do we keep our work clothes on or litter them across our home? How many times have we taken work home? And worked in front of the TV, beside the bed, or on the dining room table? The subconscious mind now has difficulty separating work and home activities. So there is a part of us that stops us fully unwinding and relaxing when we arrive home because we have 'contaminated' our home with work. Our sleep is affected for the same reason. Home starts to lose its 'homey' feeling.

It's critical that we 'decontaminate' our house. We need to allocate one area in the house that is just for work. All our work needs to be done there and all work phone calls made from that place. If we have small homes or need to spread out, cover the dining table with a cloth when working to delineate between work time and relax time. When we eat, we must uncover the table and remove all work. (Or vice versa!)

As soon as we arrive home, it helps to change into home clothes. Never work in bed again! If you take work reading to bed then your mind is focused on those issues which are not conducive to either relaxing or relating to your partner. It doesn't really boost your sex drive either. Bed is for sleeping, relaxing and other stuff – not work.

If you work in front of the TV, always have a 'working chair' and a 'relaxing chair'. When you finish working, immediately swap to the relaxing chair. Be very precise and rigid about this or you will contaminate the relaxing chair!

Think of other ways you could set your house up as a stress-free zone. We may need to decontaminate our car, so that at weekends we remove all traces of work items and the car is then ready for fun.

Maybe we could have one or two special outfits for those really tense days – something comfortable and loved that makes you feel more relaxed and reminds you of good times. The subconscious mind loves symbols and rituals – use them to your best advantage.

Find a place that recharges your batteries: the beach; a lake; a mountain retreat; a lush, green park. It needs to be the kind of place you walk away from feeling refreshed and revitalised. Visit it often!

What about making a stress-free centre at work? Nominate one place that has a great view, or feel, or has something special about it. When you go to this spot, deep breathe and consciously relax. After a while of consciously letting go, your bodymind will take over and relaxation begins to happen automatically whenever you go to this spot. Eventually all you will have to do is just look at it or think about it: your body chemistry will change, and you will calm down. See, it's easy!

7

disconnection

Because we live with such a materialistic view of life, many of us expect solutions to be expensive, complicated, time-consuming and difficult to do. Not always so with stress! There are lots of simple, quick steps we can take to temporarily restore our physiology (body chemistry) to balance.

One of the most effective was brought to my attention by my masseur, who practices shiatsu blended with some special hidden healing talent. We were discussing causes of depression and stress and her belief was that people who were 'disconnected' from friends, family, loved ones or life in general were those who felt depressed, sad or stressed.

The more I thought about this the more I realised how right she was. To keep us going at the pace many of us travel, we simply don't make time to connect with others. We glance past them, like an insect that skips onto the surface of a pond and then immediately lifts off again. We might 'connect' several times but each visit is just a fleeting second – not enough time to make real contact.

We might see our best friends only once a month or once every three months; our parents or family less often; our life partners we might see every night but we gradually spend more time at work and less time at home. We might even bring work home or work on weekends, tearing more precious moments away from 'connecting time'.

Which is the concept I want to introduce! Connecting time.

I know it sounds a bit corny, but unless we have someone bring it to our attention pre-crisis, some dramatic event will force us to recognise that being connected to someone or something special is a vital life force and a source of great energy, vitality, comfort and peace.

So how much 'connecting time' do you have a week? And don't talk about how, as a couple, you have minimal time together but when you do, it's 'quality time'. You need *quantity* time together to maintain a healthy relationship – with life partners, children and friends.

How connected to your partner are you? to your children? to your family and friends? How much do you know about their lives at this moment? about how they are really feeling about things? about their fears, concerns, challenges and joys? about the dreams, goals and desires they have, and what you could do to help or guide them? How comfortable are you just being with them – not necessarily doing anything specific, just 'mooching' about, being in the same room with them?

And how much energy do you give them? How much of yourself have you shared with them? Connection is a two-way street – we can plug into them but we have to allow them to plug into us to be really connected at a deep level. What do they know of you, your feelings, fears, dreams? Do they know where you are at the moment? And if it's a limited knowledge, is it because they failed to show interest or because you didn't let them grow close enough to discover the real you?

Come to think of it, how connected are you to yourself? It's very difficult to live our lives not only disconnected from others but out of touch with ourselves as well! In neurolinguistic programming (not a new form of pasta but a different way of looking at how people communicate), we talk about being dissociated and associated. Being associated means we are emotionally 'in there'. We are in our bodies, experiencing the actions, sensations and feelings that go with living life. It's like virtual reality but it actually is reality. (I can't believe that I'm using a 'techno' term to help people better understand what used to be inner knowing!)

Being dissociated means we are 'outside' ourselves. We can metaphorically observe ourselves as we go through situations in life, sort of like watching ourselves on a TV screen instead of being in the movie.

Being in our body, in the movie and experiencing the thoughts, emotions and actions is associated and connected. Watching the movie detaches us from ourselves and others, so we don't experience the emotions as strongly – or at all.

Life often appears easier to live from a dissociated place. There seem to be fewer highs and lows, fewer emotional roller coasters. But it's only appearance. Short-term dissociation is a very useful strategy to help us deal with a time of crisis. Long-term dissociation leads to possible disconnection from our life-lines. We move away from those we love and who love us; we pull down shutters, build barriers, distance ourselves, become aloof – all because we want to protect ourselves. What we don't realise is we are doing the opposite – we are making ourselves targets for depression, stress and misery.

How do you function most of the time? Associated or dissociated? Connected or 'lost in space'? We all have the ability to switch between the two states and we usually balance them. It's when one or the other state becomes a permanent habit that our problems may begin. Living life mostly dissociated may be safer, but it may also be dangerous for ourselves and others. Being permanently associated is often emotionally draining.

As a general rule, it's wonderful to be associated with magic moments in our lives – moments of great fun and joy and love. And it's smart to be dissociated from moments of great trauma.

Begin to notice how you are experiencing life. Make a commitment to notice where you are four times a day; or catch yourself in the middle of a situation and see if you are associated or dissociated. (You have to momentarily dissociate to notice this if you are right 'in there' experiencing the moment!)

Spend some time thinking about how connected you are. And with whom. Especially with yourself. Do you know how you feel about all sorts of people and things? Do you know what you like, want and need to stay happy? Talk to others about this concept of deep connection to others, or pets, or causes, or communities or a purpose in life. A deep connection to work is OK if it doesn't disconnect you from others and the rest of your life.

If you are not connected to someone or something, you might feel lost, unfulfilled, unhappy, depressed, and that life has no meaning.

Better get connected, it'll open up your world. Like the Internet. But it's better than the Internet – it's free!

PS: Being connected on the Internet doesn't count. It's the ultimate in dissociation from humans.

8

it's all in the mind

While preparing for this article, it dawned on me that the simplest way to achieve wellness was to balance stillness and stimulation. We live in a society bombarded with stimulation, whether it's from TV (although some would question the level of stimulation from TV!), computers, work, meetings, politics, high-speed travel, movies, videos, the fast pace of all aspects of life, the speed of information discovery or just our own minds.

And of course we all need some degree of stimulation or we would be plants! But we rarely need the level that accosts us every day. In fact, not only do we not need it but it is potentially harmful. And often useless. Worry is focusing on things we don't want to have happen.

Why do so many of us ignore precious moments of wonderful sunshine and gentle breezes or the company of loved ones as those moments are happening, and replace them with nagging doubts, anxiety or just plain fear about things that are unlikely to happen anyway? If you have developed a habit (because that's all it is) of forgetting the pleasant present to focus on an unpleasant possible future (or even worse, the past), try this technique: mindfulness. It's simple, cheap and easy. The trick is remembering to practise it.

Mindfulness is when we stay aware of what is happening to us, our feelings or what we notice around us at every moment. It helps us stay focused on the present and, God forbid, even enjoy the moment! It means keeping our absolute attention on what we are doing right now.

Or you could try an even more simple technique – try it before you scoff because it really works! Put a loose rubber band around your wrist and every time you notice yourself worrying about something, pull the rubber band out as far as you can and let it go! Yes, it will hurt. That's the point. You brain is not stupid and learns quickly. If every time you have a negative or worrying thought you snap the old wrist, you will soon stop having those anxiety-causing thoughts. Your wrist may bleed a little but the results are worth it! This technique gets rid of worry but it's still a good idea to practise mindfulness.

Stilling our mind is what most of us need to feel more peaceful. There are many ways to do this and in my opinion one of the best is to meditate.

Meditation is just a word that means training your mind to think of only one thing at a time. This is a remarkably simple-sounding task and yet extraordinarily challenging for most people. It can be done either with a relaxation tape, or by sitting quietly and repeating a single word like 'calm' or 'one' or 'white' or 'flow' (or any word you want); or focusing on your breathing in and out; or learning TM (transcendental meditation); or daydreaming; or mountain climbing; or sitting in the garden and focusing on nature until you feel better. Make sure you do this for 20 minutes every day – it's even better if you do it twice a day.

The benefits are extraordinary – much more energy and vitality; high-quality sleep; improved creativity; less stress; more productivity; enhanced performance; improved health and a stronger immune system; improved communication and relationships and on and on the benefits go! It's better than sleeping because our brain waves fall to deeper levels during meditation than in sleep, and this deeply relaxes our mind and allows our body to self-repair.

So there's a lot to be said for stillness of the mind.

But what about those whose brains have been too still for

too long? Or a suddenly retired brain? They need stimulation. Mental exercise is just as critical as physical exercise. So dash out and learn something new! Learning is fertiliser and nutrition and water and food for our brain – it loves learning! Anything. Go and study a new language, the piano, carpentry, art appreciation, literature, cooking, massage, gardening, reflexology or cars or boats, how to play chess, bridge – anything you think you might like. And if you don't like it, try something different. You'll never run out of things to learn.

Of course brains that have suffered too much of the same stimulation (subtle word for *work*) desperately need to have stillness *and* a different form of stimulation. That's where hobbies, sport or learning new skills comes in. Go to the library and read voraciously. Play on the Net and see what you can find. Do volunteer work. Build something. Write novels. Laugh. Go to acting classes. Do something you've always wanted to experience. Get your thrills from new skills!

Above all, have fun. A wellness mind and life is all about balancing stillness and stimulation and the types of stimulation – and savouring every moment!

9

unwind before you arrive home

Picture this scenario: you are at work, having a pig of a day. Everything seems difficult, nothing is going smoothly, and you can't seem to get ahead or make any impact on your in-tray. Suddenly, you notice it's 6.30 p.m. Damn! You promised to be home early tonight. You fly to the car, drive like a maniac to get home as soon as possible and walk in the door. Only to be greeted by lots of noisy family members wanting your attention.

It's the last thing you need or want. So you raise your voice, act irritated and ask everyone to leave you alone for ten minutes so you can change and unwind. You then proceed to have a dreadful evening with everyone upset, irritated, picky or sulking.

In the last month I have presented at about fifteen conferences and this particular issue has raised its head an unusual number of times. People are commenting on how hard it is to leave work at work, and arrive home and immediately become the 'home/family person'.

Both men and women have said the same thing and it appears to be really interfering with their quality of life. They arrive home, are snappy, irritable, uncommunicative, withdrawn, focused on work problems and generally bad company. And the next thing that happens – yes, you guessed it – a fight! Soon, it's the normal state of affairs (so to speak!) at which point we decide it's all too hard and we separate, and start the whole process over again.

We really can't expect our partners and children to leave us alone for fifteen minutes after we arrive home just so we can unwind in peace. They are excited about our arrival! And children don't understand the need to unwind.

We need to think about what we can do to leave work at work, and have our minds and hearts as well as our bodies at home when we are there.

Step one is to just be aware that we bring work problems home. Sometimes we don't realise that our behaviour is different, that we are being difficult, unreasonable and all those other words our loved ones are calling us! Perhaps you could pay attention to your behaviour in the first half hour after you arrive home. How do you communicate? Do you dive for the television (and go deaf)? Disappear for a run or walk? Or do you make a point of giving your partner and/or children your full attention for fifteen minutes, listening (really listening) to them and what they did and then doing your 'thing'?

Step two is to think about what sorts of things help us relax and leave the stresses and problems of work behind. Here's a list of strategies that work well – if you don't have a routine of your own, maybe one of these could be a starting point for you.

- Have a notebook and pen in the car and, as soon as you climb into the car, write down all the things you need to attend to the next day and prioritise them. Or list the problems facing you and their possible solutions. Or list the issues that have been worrying you and rate them in order of significance. Then close the notebook and put it in the console or the glove box – and that marks the end of your work day.

  From that point on you focus on home, good things that have happened to you, or something you could look forward to at home. If your mind slips back to work, gently tell yourself that work is in the glove box and you'll take the page out the next morning, when it's time to think about work again. Surprisingly, it takes only a short time before your brain learns that the notebook going into the glove box is a sign to change to home thinking or feeling.

- Use a geographical marker on the way home to signal to your brain that work thinking stops here and home feeling starts. In Sydney, some people use the two pylons on the Sydney Harbour Bridge. As they drive past the first one, they know they have only the time it takes to reach the other one before they regiment their brain to stop work thinking. Do you have any markers you could use?

- Stop at some scenic or quiet spot on the way home (not the pub!) and take your ten minutes to unwind there. Take off an article of clothing that represents work, like your tie if you're a bloke (or a tie-wearing woman) or your work shoes, and put 'home shoes' on. Then take 10 minutes to meditate (no, you don't have to sit in a corner in orange robes chanting 'om'!) – all you do is stare at the view and think of nothing; or focus on your breathing in and out, in and out; or focus on your muscles, notice any tension and release it; or repeat the word 'flow' to yourself; or focus on a colour or sound; or any one of a zillion things like that. This helps your mind to settle and leave the jangled chaos of work thinking behind.

- Play a cassette on the way home. If you have a favourite piece of music, tape it. Sometimes it helps to have faster music at the beginning of the tape to match the faster pace of your 'work brain' and slow it down gradually over a period of ten or fifteen minutes, so that by the time you arrive home you have slowed down.

- Or listen to a comedy tape, or a tape of laughter – infectious laughter that will make you grin, if not laugh! Or play motivational tapes or personal development tapes – no work ones!

- Or listen to a fun radio station – not news programmes. All the news does is give you something else bad on which to focus.

- Plan your next holiday. Think about what you would do, how relaxed you'd be and how much fun you would have.

This is just a small list of the possible ways to unwind before you arrive home so you can start the night off the way you would like it to finish. Enjoy!

10

psychoadrenalin

One of the perks of my job is the chance to meet fascinating people like Olympic medal-winner Kieren Perkins. When I heard Kieren speak, he made a comment that stuck in my mind. In the three hours before his gold-winning performance he sat alone and prepared himself mentally for the task ahead. Recognising that he was anxious and knowing the effect 'psychoadrenalin' would have on him, he was determined to regain his mental control, focus and positive mental attitude. Which obviously he did – in a stunning, gold-medal way!

It was the first time I had heard the word 'psychoadrenalin'. He knew that if he let himself stay fearful, that state of mind would keep his system full of stress chemicals ('psychoadrenalin') which would exhaust him before he'd even reached the starting blocks.

How many times do you feel exhausted and you haven't really done anything physical to cause that exhaustion? Or you feel drained of all energy and vitality? I think it might be the old 'psychoadrenalin'.

And just when you thought it was safe to feel stressed . . . American researchers are changing our thinking. It appears that a stressful experience does not just initiate a burst of chemicals which then fade away. It seems to change us, to actually alter the way our bodies and brains function.

We have known for a long time that prolonged stress destroys our immune system and plays havoc with most of our body systems (especially the gut, lungs, adrenal glands and heart); that it damages our blood cells and precipitates strokes; it affects our memory and moods (by altering brain chemicals like serotonin); and that it is a precursor to rheumatoid arthritis. Other than those effects, stress isn't too bad!

In other words, we can fool our minds but we can't fool our bodies. Our bodies react physiologically to stress, releasing stress hormones, even if our mind says, 'We're OK'! Of course, it helps to be realistic in response to a situation – rather than reacting with panic and mentally screaming, 'OH NO!'. Which immediately sends the body into 'red alert' mode. But denying how we feel doesn't work either – our bodies are too smart.

But wait, there's more. It now seems that our body becomes sensitised to stress, so that while our mind thinks everything is cool, our body thinks the 'end is nigh'. Michael Meaney of McGill University suggests we find ourselves in a mildly stressful situation, recognise it mentally as mild stress, and despite that, our body still goes berserk (my paraphrasing). In other words, we are responding totally inappropriately. And our actual brain circuits change. Oh oh.

Even anticipating a stressful situation, regardless of whether it turns out that way, sends a stress-sensitised body into a frenzy and pumps it full of brain- and body-destroying stress chemicals. It also appears that childhood stress has an impact on our future reactivity to stressors. Double 'oh oh'.

If all this is true (and it seems to be validated by loads of university professors researching in the area of stress), then we need to make some changes very fast.

What can we do? Intersperse your day with a number of unobtrusive 'stress-busters' before you feel stressed.

The following are some subtle stress-busters you may choose to practise. They might seem too simple and easy to be effective, but they are great ways to actually change your physiological makeup and neutralise the stress chemicals.

1. Take two deep breaths (filling up the base of your lungs, not

just heaving your shoulders up high) every time you look at the phone or just before you answer it.

2. Focus completely on the task at hand and eliminate self-talk (you know, the trillion words passing through your mind every minute that are telling you that you are hopeless or helpless or useless, etc).

3. Stop and stare out the window and think of nothing for two minutes every two hours (set your watch).

4. Close your eyes and cover them with your palms for one whole minute every hour (extraordinarily relaxing).

5. Stand up and stretch every joint in your body every hour.

6. In situations when you would normally respond with a huge internal 'OH NO', catch yourself and instead say, 'Oh, that's interesting!' Sounds stupid but really works!

7. Make sure you have some sort of lunch break and go outside, even if it's only for ten minutes.

8. Relive a funny or pleasant experience or look at a photo of happy times.

9. Find a favourite fun song like 'Always look on the bright side of life' from Monty Phython's *Life of Brian*, and sing it to yourself every couple of hours.

10. Whistle as you walk from office to office or meeting to meeting (this makes people wonder what's happening in your life and why you're so chirpy!).

These are just a few of the millions of effective little stress-busters you can use – strategies that bust stress, boost energy and stop that nasty sensitisation process.

11

stress-busters 2

The truth is out – stress speeds up the aging process! It seems that it's better to bust stress in small bits during each day rather than hanging out as a walking stress-ball until our annual three-week holiday. It's on the cards that if you live this way, you will be sick the whole holiday anyway, only to recover when it's time to return to work!

If this is the story of your life, then plan your days around some of the following stress-busting strategies.

Buy one of those ceramic or glass oil-burner kits – one with a deep dish for the oil and water so it will last most of the day – and a supply of nine hour candles. Add to your shopping list good quality aromatherapy oils like lavender, bergamot and orange. Then add a couple of drops of oil to the dish of water, light the candle and place your mobile stress-buster kit near your desk. Breathe deeply every half hour. There are aromatherapy oils to relax you, to enhance your creativity, to stimulate you, to lift your spirits – in fact, there's an aromatherapy oil for nearly everything!

Take a walkman with you to work after you have made a tape of all your favourite comedy skits – Bill Cosby or Billy Connolly or *Mr Bean* (not easy on audio cassette!) or anyone that makes you laugh, or even smile. And every couple of hours, take a five-minute break and listen to a skit. Hopefully it will make you laugh or smile, which will increase your endorphin (the body's natural happy hormone) level, which in turn makes you feel good. Play another comedy tape to and from work, or a laughter tape, or a tape of beautiful, soothing music.

If there is a video machine, take a *Mr Bean* or *Absolutely Fabulous* or any of your favourite comedy videos to work and play them at lunch. Or once a week in the evening, take out a new comedy video and gather the whole family to watch and laugh together.

Have a problem or issue book at work – a simple writing book will do. Every time you find yourself worrying about issues that are not related to your immediate work, write them down in this book so you can, at a later time, refer to your scribblings and spend serious time worrying about what you wrote down. You'll be surprised at how many of your worries vaporise between the time you wrote them down and the time you decided to worry about them!

Smile. That's all you need to do to trigger the release of endorphins. Even if you bare your teeth in a forced grin, your brain can't tell the difference between that and a real smile. As long as you pull your lips apart and show all your teeth, your brain (happily) interprets this as a grin, which sends a message to your brain, which cools down the hypothalamus (part of your brain), which then sends this message to the rest of your brain: 'They're smiling, send endorphins!'

In fact, you don't even have to smile. All you have to do is put a pen or pencil between your teeth – make sure your lips are not touching the pen. Your brain will interpret this as a grin and bingo – endorphins will start flowing! I know you are thinking to yourself that this is rubbish – but it's true. I have had sales people do this as they drive from client to client and they claim it works! It works for me too. Try it next time you're working on a document – you dribble a little but you feel better!

Think of anything that calms you. How about repeating the word 'calm' silently to yourself for five minutes? Or finding a quiet spot away from the phone for a couple of chest-loosening breaths? Or exchange jokes with another stress-relief seeker. Or hear your favourite soothing music silently in your head. Or play it out loud if it's acceptable to your work mates. Think of and relive past tranquil moments. In your mind, go to your favourite calming hideaway and spend a couple of minutes there absorbing the calm.

Find, or create, a symbol of calmness for yourself: something that when you look at it immediately reminds you to stop, relax and breathe. Perhaps it could be a photograph of your children laughing; you laughing; you on your last holiday; a silly moment at dinner; your favourite place – whatever works for you. Or some other symbol like my favourite – a bungy-jumping sheep I collected on my last trip to New Zealand. It sticks on a wall and as you throw it out, it makes a baaaaaa noise and everyone laughs! (Even brilliant minds need some relief!)

Do some shoulder rolls – great big circles in both directions. People don't realise how tense their neck and shoulders become after hours of sitting at a desk, or even minutes in a tense situation, whether it's a meeting or a phone call. Consciously stretch your arms out above your head and arch backwards over the chair.

Be aware of your jaw. Is it clenched? Are your teeth grinding slowly away? Make a conscious effort to loosen your jaw. Move your lower teeth from side to side. Press your fingers into your jaw joints and massage them until they loosen up.

Make a list of the stress-busting strategies that work best for you and pin it to your office or kitchen wall. Check each day that you have done at least two from the list – and you know that you have just slowed down your aging process. Who knows – if you do this often enough, you might even have a whole holiday without being sick!

12

sickness and stress

Most people today are stressed out of their minds! It doesn't matter if you work at an office, factory or home. And the bad news is . . . we can fool our minds but we can't fool our bodies. So we may go on for twelve months rushing, living at a frantic pace and surviving without becoming sick during the year. But as soon as we go on holidays our bodies sigh, 'Thank goodness, at last I've got time to be sick!' So we are!

There's even more bad news. Most of us think that we can ignore our needs to balance out some of the stress with exercise, good food, relaxation and pampering ourselves – *wrong*! There is a frighteningly large body of evidence that links the onset of horrible diseases like cancer, rheumatoid arthritis, chronic fatigue syndrome and multiple sclerosis to a very stressful period eighteen months to two years before.

Because this is so important, let me put it another way. If you are going through a really stressful, difficult time or have been for some time; if people who know you well or love you start mentioning you are very tense/short-tempered/different; if you get sick consistently on holidays; if your personality changes on holidays – then you need to take regular relaxation breaks.

When you think you have less time than you've ever had to take these breaks, then that is when you need them the most.

Cancer is a lifestyle disease in many cases. Most of the serious illnesses that really destroy our lives are. So please review what's happening to you now; or what has been happening over the last two years. If it's been really tough for you and/or very stressful, it's never too late to start pampering yourself; be much more focused on you, and on what you need to do to unwind and let go of all the stuff you have been pushing down and storing in your body.

Most people, when they take time to sit and think about what they are feeling and what they need, know the answer. We normally don't take time to think along these lines, or let our souls catch up with the rest of us.

And then we need to think of all the 'ill feelings' (think about how that term came to be!) we are harbouring. Hate, hostility, aggression, anger, resentment or unforgiveness sit in our bodies and, almost literally, 'fester', causing disease. Especially unforgiveness. It's really important we recognise these feelings and do something about releasing them or letting them go in whatever way is appropriate for us.

The longer we carry them around (and many people aren't even conscious that they are still carrying them), the more damage we do. There are already scientific studies for example, that link anger – particularly hostility – to heart attack. So it's not all mumbo jumbo 'new age' stuff!

Anyway, back to the connection between a stressful time two years before a serious illness. Perhaps we should make a scale for ourselves – evaluate our normal (before the big pressure time) daily life and grade it. Then decide how much we need to do to counterbalance the normal load. Now think of our lives with extra pressure and decide how much more we need to do to counterbalance the excessive load.

Maybe we make a promise to ourselves that if we get through the next two months, we will take four days off and do nothing. THEN DO IT – we must not make contracts with ourselves and not fulfil them! The body remembers and if you continually make contracts and then fail to take the promised breaks, it will finally do something to force you to stop! Via illness, back pain, ulcers, accidents, and so on.

I know that I have just increased your stress levels because you are now thinking, 'Oh my goodness, it's too late!' or 'How can I fit anything else into my day? It'll be more stressful trying to do that than just work!'

It's time to adjust our thinking! Our bodies are too important to be ignored or taken for granted. So it's never too late – just do more unwind activities to counteract longer stress periods. Initially it may seem more stressful trying to insert an activity just for you into your day. But soon the rewards you reap will make it the best part of your day, as well as giving you more energy, and improving your ability to focus and concentrate.

13

misery contests

How many people greet you each day – or even once in their lives – with 'Hi, what's the best thing that's happened to you today?' Not many, I bet. And if they did, what would your reaction be? Shock? Would you stand there, stunned?

It appears to me that many people are out there to have misery contests! You know the sort of person – when you ask, 'Hi – how are you?' they reply with, 'Not so good. The dog died, my piles are bad, the house needs painting, the children have got measles and my car broke down.' Which immediately prompts you to respond with as many things you can think of that went wrong over the same period and before you know it you're embroiled in a 'go for the throat' misery contest. You felt quite good when you met them but you feel suicidal now!

So be wary of those who greet you with misery and negativity. For whatever reason, they can drag most of us down. Just for one week don't ask everyone you meet, 'How are you?' They never answer with the truth anyway! They always say, 'Fine, thank you' while their body language says 'Terrible!' Instead ask, 'What's the best thing that's happened to you since I last saw you?' And watch their faces as they progress through, 'What?' to 'What *was* the best thing?' Then see their faces light up as they remember the good things and temporarily forget the rest.

If you find a person who can't remember anything good that happened, maybe you are doing them a big favour. You may be the trigger that starts them looking at life in a more positive way.

It doesn't matter if people think you are a little mad. They'll get used to it if you do it regularly. In fact, if they know you will be doing this, they'll probably start saving up 'good' events so they have something to talk to you about.

What if you made it routine at the dinner table to ask each other, 'What's the best thing that happened to you today?' – imagine the response! Knowing that you would be asked this question each night could make you focus and look for the good things during the day. It's a great habit to help your children develop. We may complain about our children being lethargic or unmotivated but what do we model for them? Are we happy and motivated over dinner or are we complaining and being miserable ourselves?

Looking for good events each day, no matter how small, or recognising and appreciating moments of joy, changes the whole calibre of our days. It shifts the focus of our minds and makes us energy-givers.

Have you ever noticed how some people you meet leave you feeling great and re-energised? And others come along and 'suck you dry', somehow draining your energy so that you feel like a washed-out rag? If these people won't become more positive, then avoid them! And hang out with positive types who are willing to dwell on the good things rather than the misery.

What do you think about just before you go to bed? Most of us worry about the things that are not going well or that have gone wrong that day – and we can stay awake for hours afterwards. And feel terrible in the morning. Just before bedtime, why not count the number of good things that happened to you that day? Think about them for a while and you'll be asleep before you know it.

Become a competitor in the 'How many good things happened to you today?' contest, avoid those misery contests, and you'll feel better, have made friends, live longer and laugh more!

14

sudden illness

There is no such thing as a sudden heart attack. It takes years of preparation and effort!

What is your lifestyle preparing you for in future years? Very few people have some *sudden* illness or disease or back pain or neck pain or ulcers. Years of preparation have gone into the development of these disorders. And usually years of ignoring warning signs from our bodies.

Imagine you are a child who is in the physical and mental shape you are now in and actually living exactly the way you are living right now. What advice would you give them? As you think about this lifestyle, observe the child's (ie your) life and emotional, mental and physical states. How happy are they? How fulfilled? challenged? stimulated? appreciated? popular? happy? balanced? Or are they sad? frightened? alone? worried? Do they have low energy or enthusiasm?

Let me define the concept of 'living' because I think lots of people are actually unaware that they 'died' some years ago. Their spirit and zest for life died anyway. They live 'life' in a rote, routine, boring, depressed way. They take everything that happens desperately seriously – especially themselves! And they make everything a crisis or a life-threatening experience. Life has no laughter – just occasional sniggers.

Real living is when we wake up with some energy and enthusiasm for the coming day. When we are excited by new ideas and concepts and opportunities to learn. When we have moments of great contentment. Or some contentment anyway. When we accept others and ourselves and enjoy the differences. When we take sensible risks that help us grow. When we laugh lots – especially at ourselves. When we see the positive aspects of others and of situations rather than focusing on the negative. When we take responsibility for ourselves and take control over what we can in our lives. When we make an effort to see friends and maintain relationships. When we treat ourselves and our loved ones with great respect. When we have a higher purpose than just making it through to the next day. When we help or try to help others. When we can make worthwhile contributions to the community or others less fortunate than ourselves. When we are thrilled by beautiful scenery or music or poetry. When we can feel emotions. When our bodies feel healthy and flexible and alive.

So what advice would you give your child?

What lifestyle and emotional changes would you gently encourage them to adopt? How would you suggest they motivate themselves to make the changes they need to make? How could they incorporate these changes into each day with an easily manageable programme? Could you suggest a timetable that gradually incorporated a series of changes? How important is it that your 'child' begin some of these changes soon?

What would you say was the highest priority to change? How would the child know if the changes were working? What benefits would they see? What would happen to them if they continued their current lifestyle? I'm sure that you, as a caring and loving parent, could think of lots more questions to ask this child. And lots more help and advice you might like to give this child.

And perhaps you might help them understand the importance of looking after themselves on a weekly basis rather then waiting until they find themselves with a major illness to make the changes. And you might suggest they keep events in perspective – are most events really crises? Or could they view them in a different way – a more realistic way?

Sudden illness doesn't happen very often – unless you are hit by a truck. And even then, was it sudden or a result of you being tired or stressed and not paying attention? Most illnesses that affect us today are created by consistently poor lifestyle habits or by us ignoring our wellness needs; by not keeping things that happen to us in perspective and not unwinding from hectic lives.

What are you doing on a daily basis to create that *sudden* illness? And what are you doing on a daily basis to *avoid* that *sudden* illness?

attitude
happiness

1

attitude adjustment hour

Most of us would be familiar with the term 'attitude adjustment hour' used by many pubs and hotels to promote their half-price drinking session between 5 p.m. and 6 p.m. Alcohol certainly can have a dramatic influence on our attitude – not always positively, of course. However, the concept of the attitude adjustment hour is great.

What is 'attitude', anyway? The dictionary defines it as 'posture of the body; settled behaviour as showing opinion'. The thesaurus uses these words: stance, type, kind, pattern, frame of mind, mood. So that clarifies it, doesn't it? Ha, ha!

It seems to me that attitude refers to the way we perceive things in life. It's the filter through which we sift all information. The 'glasses' through which we look at the world. The way we taint, colour or tint what we see, hear and consequently feel. And it's a choice – we can choose the glasses we want.

Our posture reflects how we feel – we stand upright and ready to face what comes when we feel 'up' or positive; or slouched with our eyes looking down when we are negative or 'depressed'. We are not sure if mood follows posture or posture follows mood – so until we are sure, if you feel down, make an effort to stand tall and look up and I bet it improves your mood.

People who have a 'good' attitude take responsibility for themselves and for what happens to them and are usually fun to be around. They can turn situations around and see the positive side; they view mistakes as learning; they choose to avoid people who drag them down; they are optimistic and expect good things to happen to them; they see the best in others.

'Poor' attitude people blame others for their circumstances and are stress or depression carriers. They will turn the best situation into one that is negative, and see mistakes as massive failures and as proof that they personally are failures. These are the people who worry if they have nothing to worry about. They hang about other negative people and if you are feeling good they will try to point out why you should not! They expect the worst – and usually get it. Avoid them – at all costs.

We used to hear about people's attitude problems; now we just hear that someone has 'an attitude', which means they have an attitude problem.

So the concept of an attitude adjustment hour is great! What if we set aside a period of time each day to review our current attitude, the way we are viewing the world, and change it if we need to?

For example, at the end of the day, do you arrive home tense and in 'hurry mode'? Even if you don't think you do, you probably do! Ask your partner and children (who are brutally honest) if your fuse is short when you come home or if you are irritable or if your behaviour is any different from holiday behaviour. This should give you valuable information about how much you unwind on the way home, and whether you need to adjust your attitude.

I wonder if it might be a good exercise to have a few attitude adjustment moments during the day. Perhaps on the way to work or when driving anywhere, become conscious of what you are thinking about work and your day. Do you have a positive or negative attitude? Are you feeling enthusiastic or bored? And what sort of attitude or thinking could you choose instead?

And before those cynics out there cry, 'No more of this "positive" garbage!', let me add that people who are positive in their outlook have better health, live longer, recover from disease more quickly, are more popular and suffer less stress. Other than that, being negative is just fine!

On reflection, it's pretty easy to change your attitude to the weather. When I lived in a unit with no garden, I used to hate rain. I would curse it and become irritable. After I bought a house and garden, I'd wake up to find it's raining and think, 'Hooray! I don't have to water today'. So we can change our attitudes very quickly. If we want to.

Spend a few minutes at lunchtime listening to yourself and the quality of your thoughts. How is your attitude?

One of the huge problems with having a negative, defeatist or victim mentality (another word for attitude) is that it somehow radiates out of your body and other people pick up on it. This shows up in meetings and corporate settings as much as in the home environment.

Be careful, you may infect your children with the 'negative attitude' virus which could affect their whole lives. You are certainly gifting your child a 'filter', like a pair of glasses that can be rose-coloured or black. Everything the child sees through your eyes will be coloured the way you see it, and that's the way children learn to view the world.

Even though some people might feel we have no control over what we are thinking, we do! The first step is to become aware of what we are saying to ourselves at any time. When we wish to change the text in a computer document we can delete and retype, or just type over. Similarly, in our minds we can 'type over' the thoughts we would like to replace, with preferred language.

Then there is your attitude to yourself. Do you like yourself? What about your body image? Do you need an attitude adjustment on your self-image or perception of yourself?

Why not try an attitude adjustment hour (not in the pub!) once a week, and then have 'attitude adjustment minutes' throughout every day. Stop, listen to your thoughts and images, replace them with more appropriate ones and then look for the difference in your life.

Even if you think this idea sucks – try it, it works!

2

reframing

Have you ever owned a painting or photograph that has been reframed? When we change the colour of the mounting cardboard or the texture of the frame the difference can be amazing. It's the same picture but it looks totally different.

Paintings can be transformed with different colours, textures and styles of surrounds. Our minds are the same. We can 'reframe' situations, experiences and feelings just with the way we package or wrap the original memory.

This is one of the many very effective techniques of neurolinguistics and other psychological disciplines highlighted in a book called *We Are All Self Employed* by Cliff Hakim. It's well worth reading and will reframe the way you view your work and life.

How we look at events and the world is a choice. People who survived concentration camps (like Victor Frankel, author of *Man's Search For Meaning*) chose to think differently from the others despite the same physical and psychological hardships and torture.

My wonderful shiatsu massage friend, Cate, is the master of reframing. I'll go to see her once a week – as often as I hope you are having a massage – and if I happen to run through the dramas of the past few days, with a couple of words she changes the whole meaning of my grumbles (without realising she's doing it).

For example, I might be gently grumbling about all the flying I have to do and she simply says, 'The view must be beautiful from a plane as you're flying into Sydney,' or, 'It must be good to have that uninterrupted time with no phone calls to distract you,' or, 'What an opportunity to get above everything that is happening to you right now and escape for a short while.'

She helps me look at what's happening to me from another angle, with a different coloured border, so that the new perspective changes what I say to myself and consequently the way I feel.

Our patterns of thinking become habits. After a while we stop responding consciously and slip into subconscious mode – we frame most things similarly. What is your habitual pattern? Do you choose to see the up-side or the down-side of events? Do you expect the worst or presume things will all work out as they are meant to? Are you interested in reframing your experiences positively or are you happy in your own misery?

For example, do you think of mistakes as failures or view them as learning experiences? I remember reading about the managing director of a huge American company who lost a million dollars for the company as a result of a business decision he made. Called to the chairman of the board's office, he fully expected to be fired. Imagine his surprise when the chairman responded that the board didn't want him to resign – in fact, the board felt they had invested a million dollars in a training programme with him and they certainly weren't going to waste that investment!

What a wonderful reframe – from failure to huge learning opportunity! How many times in your life would it be useful to think in this way – to reframe awkward or difficult situations into useful learning experiences? And it's more than just mumbo jumbo, positive mental attitude, 'new age' stuff! How you choose to think has a direct impact on your physiology – the chemical makeup of your body. Choosing to reframe your thinking may reduce the stress response, retard aging, boost your immune system, stop cancer and chemically make you feel better.

Perhaps it would help to choose a 'starting day' – the start of your new way of approaching the world. Teach this to your children by modelling it – just behave like this and your children's attitudes will follow. The younger they are, the faster they'll follow.

Reframing is a great way to transform potential crises into manageable situations and experiences. If you are devastated by the end of a relationship, think of it in terms of a 'relating experience' rather than relationship because a relating experience implies there will be more of them and this one was just another on the journey to the best one for you.

Each day, notice the way you 'code' your experiences. If it's other than positive, try reframing what has just happened to you so that the memory to be stored is positive or at least neutral. The memories we store and the way we store them are potent causes of disease – but more of that later in this book.

In the meantime, change the colour and border of your memories and experiences and notice how your energy improves.

3

thought viruses

Robert Dilts is a well-known American expert in neurolinguistic programming who writes frequently for a magazine called *Anchor Point*. In a recent edition he was discussing the connection between beliefs and health or wellness. He introduced the concept of 'thought viruses'. What a fantastic way of describing one of the most powerful mechanisms of illness or recovery!

The link between body and mind is now proven beyond dispute. We can't always exactly define the way the two are connected but the body's influence on the mind and vice versa should be considered in the assessment of every ailment affecting us. We have a bodymind – one integrated unit. And we can sometimes fool our minds but we can't fool our bodies.

Our bodies store stress and pain and frustration, emotion and everything else! We can continue for a finite time abusing our bodies, stretching ourselves to the mental limit or stressing ourselves to the maximum, and then we start being given warning signals. If we ignore these warning signals, if we continue to push ourselves beyond a reasonable limit, if we never slow down long enough to listen to our bodies then something gives. We 'suddenly' find ourselves with a bad back or a bad neck or pneumonia or malnutrition or migraines or stomach upsets or chronic fatigue syndrome or rheumatoid arthritis or heart disease and so forth.

Michael Crichton, the author of *Jurassic Park,* originally trained as a doctor, and when he was a resident he conducted a survey of heart attack patients. Without exception, when he asked these people, 'Why did you have this heart attack?', they would give answers based on emotion, like 'My work situation was unsatisfactory – I was living with uncertainty,' or, 'My wife left me,' or, 'Our marriage was going through a difficult time,' and so on. They'd all related the illness to a mental or emotional trigger. Not to, 'I had been exercising too hard,' or, 'I carried too many boulders in the garden.'

So with this bodymind, our non-physical thoughts and beliefs and our physical bodies are interchangeable. Our thoughts can cause disease. Our body can affect our moods. (Try feeling excited and enthusiastic when you are slumped, your head dropped and eyes looking at the ground!) Lifestyle is still critical, but what determines our lifestyles if it isn't our beliefs about how we should live or how we need to live?

Beliefs are deeply ingrained thoughts about the way we feel the world does or should work. And our beliefs influence everything we see, do, hear and say. It's as though anything that comes into or out of ourselves is filtered through our belief systems which act as rose-coloured glasses or black-tinted lenses or purple glass or whichever way our beliefs colour that part of our world.

For example, 'pointing the bone' in cultures where the belief is that if the witchdoctor points a bone at you, death follows, can ensure the death of a perfectly healthy individual because they believe that they are cursed and that death is inevitable.

What happens when an expert tells a patient they have only months to live? Of course the expert is offering what they believe to be the situation based on their knowledge, experience and assessment of the person and the condition. But how many times have you heard of people who chose not to believe that 'pointed bone'? Those who decide, 'No, I will live and I'll try all sorts of ways to make me well enough to fight this condition'; someone who chooses to believe they will beat cancer? They may still make a will and organise their affairs but that's just sensible – it doesn't mean they expect to die. Even if they die, I bet they lived longer and felt more in control when they believed they could fight it.

Search your beliefs about health and wellness. Do you believe it's possible to be fit, flexible and strong when we are in our sixties, seventies and eighties? Should we keep our minds active and continue learning or does being old mean we mentally and physically shrivel up, stiffen up and die? Do you believe happiness happens to other people, not you? Or do you believe you are a depressed person – that it's just your type? Or that your father and grandfather died of heart disease, so you will? Or that bowel cancer is claiming everyone and you're next?

Why not believe that you are inherently a very well and strong person? Sit quietly and ask yourself what you need to be well – more balance; more rest; more relaxation; more stimulation; more fun and laughter; more exercise? And whatever you need, find a way of incorporating it into your life.

Believe exercise is so important that you make time for it; believe rest and meditation are too critical to miss for extended periods – if you really believe this, you will be motivated to do it.

If you have a problem or a family history of hereditary conditions then make sure you have regular checkups. Believing you are well does not mean ignoring minor or blatantly obvious signs that something is wrong – that's just being an ostrich! Seek help when you need it – your inner oracle is great most of the time but outside experts are a valuable resource.

Bacteria are individual organisms that are a form of life. Viruses are incomplete. They 'steal' from healthy parts to create a life of their own or take over the life of a healthy cell. In the same way a body or computer virus works, thought viruses insidiously slide their way into and affect or colour all our thinking. They are dangerous and quite frequently life threatening. Make sure that once a month you 'de-bug' yourself – run a 'virus checker' through your bodymind and clean it up. Delete, destroy and trash any thought viruses that are allowing your life force to weaken or ebb away.

Beware of spreading thought viruses yourself. And beware of others who are carriers of these nasty little bugs! They are more dangerous than you realise.

4

success

I have seen this poem many times and recently rediscovered it: *Success* by Ralph Waldo Emerson. It's a wonderful definition of a term that is often difficult to describe:

> To laugh often and much
> To win the affection of intelligent people
> And the affection of children;
> To earn the appreciation of honest critics,
> And endure false betrayal of friends,
> To appreciate beauty,
> To find the best in others,
> To leave the world a bit better,
> Whether by a healthy child, a garden patch
> Or a redeemed social condition,
> To know even one life has breathed easier
> Because you lived,
> This is to have succeeded.

Speaking with a friend of mine last week, the concept of success came up again. We were talking about her move away from the 'establishment'. She had left the corporate world to start her own very creative business. I asked her how she was and how her business was progressing. She sighed and said if we defined success as creating lovely items that were very saleable; as having a large database of people who wanted your treasures; and as running your own business, and covering costs, then she was very successful. But if success were defined in terms of money being earned then she was more 'successful' in the corporate world.

That started me thinking about our concept of success. It's generally not a dinner table discussion as a specific issue. It's more mentioned in passing when describing a person or venture. Or it's a word that we assume everyone understands to mean exactly what we see it to mean. Everyone knows what success is – don't they? Maybe. Maybe not.

We all have our own unstated ideas of success that we have somehow assimilated from our parents, our culture and our media/TV sources. We tend to absorb by osmosis the notion that success equals fame, bulk money and material assets. Instead, we need to rethink success, by discussing it at school, at work and at home around the dinner table.

In our society, the most widespread belief is that success, fame and money are synonymous. But are they really? How many incredibly rich, famous people are successful at being human? And are happy, with loving, supportive families, great relationships, and balanced happy children? (I know there are those out there who say, 'I've been rich and unhappy and poor and unhappy – I'll take the rich and unhappy anytime!', but maybe there's more to life than fame and money.)

What are your beliefs about success? Read Emerson's poem out to yourself and your family, friends or class and use it as the starting point for a discussion. If you have small children, discuss your ideas with your partner so that your children have the advantage of parents who have thought about this *before* they have a mid-life crisis!

If we have a sense of what success means to us, we must have considered our values. Our beliefs about success are in part determined by what we think is important in life; where we think our priorities lie. Are family and closeness important? Is massive wealth important above everything else? How much money is enough for you to feel financially secure? Is this realistic or based on some false perception we gained in childhood? Are we casting aside other important parts of our lives in the hunt for more money than we need to be well cared for?

Just one small part of my definition of success is to have achieved the financial and career goals that I set. To me, success is intricately linked to a sense of purpose and joy and happiness and contentment with ourselves and our lives, with acceptance of things the way they are and the wisdom to know what we can and cannot affect. Success is being able to enjoy moments as they happen and are, rather than wasting the present with worries of the past or fears of the future.

It's the ability to unconditionally accept ourselves and others, and to have compassion for ourselves and others and to help where we can. It's the ability to laugh at ourselves and to find things to laugh at in life, even when things are horrible. It's being excited and enthusiastic about life and learning and really living right up to the moment we die. It's about discovering more about ourselves as we mature and stretch ourselves with new skills and adventures. It's having friends that love us. And loving our friends. And our work. It's using our minds to enhance our day-to-day lives rather than fill us with woe.

What are the signs of success? To me, successful people 'glow' and sparkle with an excitement for life. They look healthy; they're enthusiastic; they sound happy and they feel content. They know they will always have challenges in life and they tackle them willingly, knowing the difficulty will pass and good times will follow; they are optimistic; they laugh a lot; they love new ideas and they love routine; they are not fanatical about anything; there are periods in their life when they are absolutely fulfilled by all the things they are doing, feeling or experiencing; they have friends who really love them and whom they really love; they have children who love them – their own or other people's; they have set realistic goals and yet still have dreams; they know mistakes equal learning rather than failure; they have fulfilled some, or all, needs in all areas of their lives.

What is your definition of success? How will you know when you are there? What will you look like, sound like, see, hear and feel when you are, by your definition, 'successful'? Think about it. Just thinking about it may have more impact than you realise!

5

age and life

I was once asked to speak at a series of seminars around Australia to people who were about to retire, or who already had. In preparing for a lifestyle presentation, I jotted down some ideas that I thought about the way older (from now on written as 'more mature') people lived in our culture.

We don't share the same sense of respect for our 'elders' as do many tribal groups and native populations. I think we should. Not everyone who is over 60 is useless! They have a wealth of knowledge that is transformed into wisdom by years of their life experiences.

Groucho Marx once advised, 'We should learn from the mistakes of others. We don't have time to make them ourselves.' And that applies even more in today's world, where we do more, with less, in less time. We should have more mature folks advising us in our lives, in small business matters – or even big business if that is what they spent a working lifetime doing. This is just one idea that jumped immediately into my mind.

I asked myself, is there life after retirement? YES! I concluded. A much better one if we prepare for it. From the age of 13 we are asked, 'What do you want to do in life?' We plan and study for twenty years for this job or work. No one mentions after work. Or makes us think about, or study for, the twenty years after we retire. We expect to find a satisfying job that makes us money and we expect to have to work until we are at retiring age, at which point we can finally start to relax and do what we want. That's the theory!

Except . . . that's not what usually happens! Especially for men and, I fear, for a growing number of women who are focusing on having a career and who will be as lost as most men who stop 'formal' work. Many men find too late that work was everything in their lives. It was stimulation, satisfaction, achievement and recognition all wrapped into one. Whew – that's a hard thing to take out of your life in one swoop. One day you're there and the next, the routine is gone; your purpose is gone; your main source of satisfaction and stimulation disappears; and you don't have any idea of how to live this new lifestyle.

So you drive your wife or partner nuts! If she hasn't been working and she is used to having the house and her days to herself, it's a rude shock to suddenly have a permanent, on-site 'helper'! Someone who wants to take over all the things that have filled her life! If you've both been working the whole time, it's a shock for both of you, although women tend to have more connections, interests and friends in life. (Of course, I'm generalising.)

We should prepare now, even if we are 27 years old, for retirement! The best preparation of all is to have a balanced lifestyle. To make sure that work doesn't consume your life: that your satisfaction, achievement and joy come from a wide range of activities. Like hobbies; learning new skills; friends; a social life; sport; the community and a sense of contributing. Learn to play bridge – it's a tremendous mental challenge. Or chess. And practice so much that you are able to compete. Fill your spare time with these pastimes so you have a balance. After all, who utters these immortal words as they draw their last breath: 'I wish I'd spent more time at work'?

Find a purpose in life other than the pursuit of financial rewards and promotion. Remember, he or she who dies with the most points still dies! If you can't think of a purpose, use the Dalai Lama's – he said the purpose of life is to be happy and useful. So get out there and be useful! Happiness follows you, rather than being the end point of a journey.

Volunteer for things. Join community groups, or groups of mature people who bushwalk or travel or meet regularly. As today's growing number of mature people seem fitter and younger looking than ever before, there are more activities being promoted for that market. Look for them. And in our working years we need to cultivate activities that we can continue in some way into our retirement time.

I met a man recently who told me that his 85-year-old mother went out to help the 'old people' by taking them Meals on Wheels. That's how I want to be.

If you're over 55, do you view yourself as old? Big mistake if you do. Think young, and that now, at last, you have the time and usually the money to do the things you want to do. Get out there and do them. Your kids don't deserve all your money. Splurge a bit for the first time in your life. Take a couple of risks now you can. Add some spice to your life with exciting holidays. Read travel books and plan a world adventure. Or go to France for a cooking class!

Exercise your mind *and* your body. Those of us who are more mature need to pump iron and build up our bodies like everyone else. In fact we need to do it more. Falls and fear come from muscle weakness more than anything – more mature people need to develop strong muscles again. Muscles are perfectly capable of being strengthened, no matter what age we are. And the stronger they are the more independent we are; the more confident we feel; and the more protected we are.

There are plenty of places now running aerobics classes for 'seniors'; consider aquarobics or exercising in the water – which is a wonderful way to start exercising if it's new to you – and to add variety to your programme if you are already fit; or start yoga – one of the world's most fantastic exercise forms! It's gentle, safe, easy, controllable and exercises brain *and* body; sports people perform much better when they incorporate the right sort of yoga into their routine. All of these exercise regimes are easier to continue than to begin for the first time, so starting before you retire is a smart move. And remember, it's never too late for exercise. At 95 I'm still going to be in that gym or lifting weights. I'll be granny Godzilla!

And if you are more mature and can't find an already organised group, start one yourself! Call gyms; find heated pools; contact senior organisations; recruit a local physiotherapist who is willing to plan and produce the programmes; start a walking group yourself; call all your friends and convince them to come with you – so that when you've finished exercising, you can all go to the local health bar and sit and drink herbal tea. Or carrot juice!

As soon as you can, learn more about your health. Read the latest research on diet, exercise, and lifestyle and it's effects on blood pressure, cancer and arthritis. Subscribe to the Life Extension Foundation, an American association that seems genuinely committed to giving out well-researched information about natural therapies that keep our brains and bodies working in peak condition until we are ready to leave life.

You have a great deal more control than you realise. When you are exercising regularly and eating well, you will be amazed at how much more energy you have; how much your moods lift and your sleeping improves; how much less your arthritis troubles you and how you need fewer drugs.

If you've been saving up all these years and focused solely on work to get the money so you could retire well, it's on the cards that you will die within the first year of retirement. Your life blood – work – just stopped. It didn't peter out or gradually fade, it just stopped. So do you! The adjustment is huge.

Prepare now. Find a balance. Develop friends. Start exercising. Have a hobby. Get a life!

6

go into the garden!

My cousin, Juliet Gore, is a natural genius! Not to mention philosopher, artist, great cook and art therapist. My visits to Adelaide are wonderful, because I often have time to see her and her equally interesting husband. As we linger over her spectacular meals, we discuss all sorts of life issues.

Last week, the topic was stress and the pace of life. We were talking about the complexity of many solutions offered to combat stress and she came up with the classic statement, 'Why don't people just go into the garden and *stay* there until they feel better'?

The more I thought about this, the more sense it made. We find ourselves in situations where we are tense, terse and testy, and we stomp around or shout at people; which gets us, and the others involved, nowhere. So what's the point? Why not escape the situation and draw breath?

Many people believe that escaping is not the answer – and in some situations it's not. But the way we live life these days often puts us in pressure scenarios in which we can't think clearly. And we say or do things we regret. Short-term escape to the garden (or metaphoric garden!) has loads of advantages.

For example, being in the garden grounds us – literally and metaphorically. We are so busy 'flying' around, doing ten things and thinking about fifty problems simultaneously, that we forget some basic principles of life. For example, we are human 'beings', not human 'doings' – we need to stop and 'be' for a while. And the garden is a really great place to just 'be'.

Make sure you go barefoot into the garden and stand on the grass – not the bricks or cement! Feel the softness of the grass underfoot – enjoy the sensation. (Make sure there are no bees, bullants, other stinging insects or prickles!) Lie down and let the warmth of the sun seep into your body – this escape is much more pleasurable on a sunny day! Wear a hat to cover your face but sun on your clothes is safe.

Breathe deeply and focus on inhaling the wonderful smells of the grass, trees and flowers. (If you suffer from hay fever, this stress-busting solution may not be the one for you!) The olfactory (smell) system has a direct and therefore powerful connection to your brains. Have you ever wandered past someone in the street who is wearing the same perfume/aftershave an old flame wore? Immediately, you are transported back to that time. Or you smell roast chicken or apple pie, and memories of Sunday lunches at Granny's place flood into your mind?

John Gray (author of *Men are from Mars, Women are from Venus*) says that it's a smart idea to wear a 'special' perfume or aftershave every time you make love to your partner. It then becomes a powerful aphrodisiac and signal to your lover when you wear it on any other occasion – as foreplay! So, take time to really develop your sense of smell.

Have you seen the spectacular ABC television series, *The Private Life of Plants*? Wonderful photography captures a fascinating world. You, too, can create your own programme – carefully examine the flowers and plants, observe the life that goes on around them. Look at how bees and other insects work with the plant kingdom to cross-pollinate. Watch the ants and determine their tasks. Find out the role of lizards in your garden. Watch the flowers opening up or closing down. Some plants you can actually watch grow!

The wonder of nature can fill another couple of hours. Look at the myriad of colours; where do those fantastic rich reds, purples, and greens come from? How do flowers come in such delicate colours, let alone such extraordinary shapes and sizes?

What about the shapes of leaves – and how do they know when to change colour? What makes branches grow where they do?

Listen to the sounds in the garden – palm leaves rustling in the wind; the hum of the wind in the trees; birds serenading each other; crickets and cicadas calling out; sometimes there appears to be silence, yet if we tune in, there is a symphony going on around us. (That was poetic for me. Must be the impact of the garden I'm sitting in as I write this!)

Gardening is a fascinating pastime. And not just for 'oldies'. Many young people I know are turning to gardening because it makes them feel so good. Not only do they find the physical work satisfying, they love to watch the fruits of their labour blossom (literally). It's like planting children and watching them grow! I know because every time one of my precious bulbs bursts forth, I get so excited, I have a mini celebration. I also wander around and talk to my plants. (I *do* have friends, it's just that I like to talk to my plants as well!)

It's also a way to develop and enhance creativity. Planning a garden, the shape, colours and sizes, and then making it happen is a terrific way of using the right side of your brain, which allows the poor old overworked left side to have a rest. You may find that you are more creative about problem-solving after a serious bout of gardening!

If you don't have a garden then do the same in a park or with pot plants. It works nearly as well. Or if the garden isn't for you, visit the beach and listen to the waves; or be embraced by a rain forest; or an isolated and nature-rich spot like Kangaroo Island.

Whatever your preference, regularly escape and recharge your batteries by immersing yourself in a favourite place. The moral of this whole article and the trick to maximising the relaxing effect is to focus completely on what is around you – and not what's going on inside you. Use all your senses – smell, see, hear, feel and taste the wonder of whatever it is around you. And, as Juliet says, stay there until you feel better!

7

something to look forward to

Somewhere in the archives of my mind I recall reading about a strategy that helped someone through a very stressful time. And I remember thinking, 'What a good idea!' This is a great technique to use when things look 'black'; when it appears that there's no way out of a mess; or when life is a boring drudge, frantically busy or stressful.

Always have something to look forward to. It doesn't matter how big or small! It's the same concept as seeing a light at the end of the tunnel. By always having something you can look forward to, you make sure the light permanently shines.

I thought it would be fun to explore the many ways we could plan this. Life is always going to come at us in waves – peaks and then troughs which usually catch us by surprise. And at the bottom of the trough where we can't see our way out, we think life is the 'pits' and we see no end to this tragedy. The anticipation of something pleasant can let us see that the sky is still above us.

It would seem smart to have both short-term and long-term events to which we can look forward. Make it a goal that at the end of this article, you will create a daily, weekly and annual series of such events.

To start this process, set up a document on your computer, buy a book or find a piece of paper you can keep somewhere special. Create separate sections that allow you to sort your ideas into daily, weekly and annual events.

Think of as many things as you can that make you feel great – any sort of activity. Dancing, reading, sewing, hobbies, singing, walking, exercising in the gym, seeing friends, romantic interludes, laughing, going to the movies, learning something new, playing the piano or other musical instrument, cooking, watching a comedy video, gardening, driving, daydreaming, doing nothing, roller blading, sailing, playing tennis or any other sport – anything that makes you feel good. Make a list of these activities (in the appropriate sections) in your special book or computer document, or on your paper.

Next, let's consider all the little things that happen in a day that might make you feel good. For example, waking up and finding out you are alive! Or watching the sunrise or sunset; watching a beautiful scene on your way to or from work; receiving a phone call from someone you love; listening to your favourite music; finishing a project; seeing your children or partner at the end of the day; having an hour to yourself – scan your days and make a list of daily 'anticipations'.

Now recall all the holidays you have ever dreamed of having. Write down all the exotic destinations – or boring ones! And describe all the sorts of things you would like to do there. Do you like beach-based holidays or outdoor adventures? Back-to-nature or exotic hotel holidays?

Or have you heard about doing wonderful things in beautiful places like cooking classes in Tuscany; walking in Nepal; 'barging' through France (this means travelling on a series of barges – not hurling yourself through masses of people!); visiting tribes in the Andes; skiing in Europe or America; camping in a game park in Africa or experiencing Egypt. Jot these down in the travel section of your book. Take time to be as descriptive as you can.

A lot of the fun of these holidays is the planning beforehand – reading all the travel guides and books on the area, and deciding what to see and experience. Discussing these details over endless dinners and cold nights, and anticipating the wonderful time you are going to have makes it all the more special.

Our brains can't tell the difference between vividly imagined experiences and reality! If we vividly recall (or relive) a wonderful experience from the past, our bodymind releases the same array of 'feel good' chemicals that it did at the time of the actual experience.

Similarly, if we vividly imagine (or pre-live) an experience that we think will be fantastic our bodyminds release feel-good chemicals! That's what daydreaming and anticipation is all about. Remember that last week at work before your holiday starts? Your body is at work but your mind is already on holiday – and you feel great!

We have extraordinary power in our bodyminds and we can release chemicals that make us 'high' at will – endorphins for example. They are much more powerful than any drug we can manufacture synthetically and can eliminate pain and make us feel fantastic. Anticipation is about imagining all sorts of wonderful scenarios and releasing these chemicals, which then make us feel great!

Having something to look forward to takes time and a little effort because we have to scan for or orchestrate these events. Sometimes they happen spontaneously – but then we didn't have the thrill of anticipation. And it's the anticipation that keeps us going through a tough time: 'I just have to last three more days and then . . .'

So this is the critical step – the planning. Each month, in your book, document or diary (for the next month at least), mark something to look forward to each day. Perhaps you can have the same one each day for a week, then have different ones for the following weeks.

Then design your weekend 'things to look forward to' for the next month. And finally the 'biggie' – the holiday! If it's not a glamorous, exotic destination, you can still imagine and plan for a wonderful time of complete relaxation, or camping or bush-walking in the country.

And you can think, dream about and plan the 'holiday of a

lifetime'. Maybe you are saving up for that trip through Europe and its castles; or a round-the-world trip. They are major 'lights at the end of the tunnel'. In fact, they are huge beacons at the end of the tunnel! It doesn't matter if this holiday isn't due to happen for ten years – it's the anticipation that makes it a fantastic stress-busting strategy.

8

be present

In dwelling, live close to the ground. In thinking, keep to the simple. In conflict, be fair and generous. In governing, don't try to control. In work, do what you enjoy. In family life, be completely present.

TAO TE CHING

The last line really made me think. Our lives today are so busy, hectic, rushed and full of concerns that we forget to *be* with our families or friends when we are with them! Of course we are there physically, but mentally we are often somewhere else.

How many times has someone who knows you well walked away mumbling that you are not listening or don't care? Or worse, walked away not saying anything – just thinking and believing that you don't care. Our non-verbal communication is 80–93 per cent of everything we communicate. Other people, especially children, know when we are not listening to them or taking in what they are saying.

One of the greatest gifts we can give the ones we love – families or friends – is to be present mentally when they are talking with us, sitting with us in quiet moments, or any time we are together.

When you come home from work, or from some activity, prepare yourself for 'being present'. As you climb out of the car, bus, plane or train, or as you are walking home, make a

138

conscious effort to say 'that's the end of work, now it's time for my other life' or 'it's time for my family or children'.

Toddlers often demand that we give them our full attention. Usually to our benefit, we are caught up in their ever-present mood of delight or wonder or complete fascination for minutes with a leaf, an ant or the wind! As children grow older they interpret our 'distance' or lack of this 'full-on attention' time as not caring. And they quietly drift away themselves. And we are so busy being busy that we don't notice we have missed our children growing up.

It's not just crucial with families. Anything we do, we can do better if we focus our full attention on it – work, tennis, reading, golf, relaxing, studying, driving. When we are on the phone to someone, they *always* know when we are doing, or thinking about, something else instead of being present with their conversation!

Our society seems to have bred a habit in us that encourages us to live in the past or in the future, so we miss all the wonderful moments we could experience every day. How many times have you realised a whole meeting has just gone by and you didn't pay attention to one word because you were thinking about the problem you had last week with your boss?

Or you arrived home in your car but have no idea of how you got there, because you were thinking about the work troubles you think you might have tomorrow? Or two hours went by at work and you didn't do a thing because you were thinking about what happened between you and your partner last night?

Can you see the benefit of being 'present' mentally and physically with everything you do? We need to live life while it's happening rather than after it did or before it does!

If we love someone, we need to give them our undivided, absolute, complete attention. Think of the first few weeks of any new romance. We notice their every move, their smell, all their little mannerisms; we study them intently! The other person loves this non-verbal caring. And we do too. We bring out the best in each other. Then time passes and other things are given more attention, more priority – usually unconsciously. We are not aware of it, but our loved ones are. And they gradually drift away.

Stop the drift. Be conscious from today onwards of where your mind is when your body is with your partner, your children, at work or relaxing. And make sure they are both together!

9

the meaning of life

More heart attacks occur at 9 a.m. on Monday morning than at any other time. This should be a cause of concern to many of us!

American research investigating factors influencing heart attack have identified a new number one peril – not cholesterol, not obesity, not lack of exercise, although they are important contributory factors, but job dissatisfaction – specifically, lack of purpose or meaning in life.

Researchers distilled dissatisfaction down to two main elements: lack of purpose or meaning in life, and a self-rating of happiness.

In other words, if someone came up to you and asked you what was your purpose in life and you looked at them as if they had two heads, and then they asked you how happy you'd rate yourself and you answered 'not very' – get medical insurance fast!

Having a purpose in life has been recognised as important by philosophers and wise people for centuries, but it seems to have escaped recognition, let alone consideration, by the bulk of our population. Perhaps we should discuss this at schools.

When the Dalai Lama visited Australia and was asked, 'What is the meaning of life?' he responded, 'To be happy and useful'.

Having some worthwhile meaning in life will make differences in the way you perceive yourself and others, and the way they perceive you.

Take time to reflect – sit and think quietly about what you could have as a purpose in your life. It doesn't matter what it is, as long as it's important to you. Mine is helping others heal and grow; to provide people with information in a simple format that they may not otherwise have access to, which then gives them more choices over what happens to them. I also want happiness and to bring joy to others and to learn and keep learning all my life. That's what I believe I'm here for.

Having a sense of what your purpose is in life is like putting a rudder on a ship. It can guide you along the path you choose. Your purpose may change as you steer your course and that's OK! The rudder just moves to a new position and you take up a new course.

I don't think this purpose has to be grand or lofty. It can be as simple as you like, as long as it means a lot to you.

What if you are stuck in a job that offers you no satisfaction? Perhaps you could decide what is missing and make some changes that would bring meaning into your work? What about pride in performing your part as an integral team member? Or just pride in what you do, no matter how trivial it may seem? Be the best 'whatever' you can be. Before you discard a job, make sure you have tried to redesign the job, or discussed changes with people who could make the changes that would give you satisfaction.

As most people spend the bulk of their waking hours at work, decide to make your work a rich source of satisfaction and meaning. What do you say to yourself about your job and the work you do? Do you recognise it as worthwhile? Or do you belittle your contribution?

Taking pride in doing your job with excellence is a start, and maybe, as you show a desire to do and be more, your job may be enlarged to give you more responsibility and authority. If you don't want more, that's great. If you are satisfied and happy with what you do, 9 a.m. Monday mornings is something to look forward to, instead of a time to die!

What if you are a home worker? I know someone who is a cleaner and this person takes fantastic pride in seeing a clean, sparkling result from what started as a mess! Perhaps you could turn your attention to the community. Do volunteer work; cheer up some lonely old people; bring joy to orphans; or just make biscuits for a disabled neighbour. Research shows that by helping other people we boost the strength of our immune systems and therefore resist disease more effectively – a bonus!

Maybe your purpose is just to be happy without hurting others, or to create a close family unit. Great! Go do it, and know you are on track.

Children benefit from being around parents who have a sense of purpose and direction. Toddlers have a fantastic sense of purpose in their lives – to learn, laugh, play, have fun, and experience as much as possible. Grown ups lose this wonderful attitude. Teenagers just get in their own way – if they had a bigger picture, a greater sense of purpose than just surviving the next few years without embarrassment, they may enjoy those precious years more.

OK, so what happens if your life is full of abuse or horror? Is there any escape? Can you find help or support? Even then, maybe your purpose is survival without scarring and to teach or help others how to do this. The classic example of how a purpose in life can sustain human beings through extreme atrocities is in Victor Frankel's book, *Man's Search For Meaning*. This man survived years in concentration camps by focusing on helping others cope, and by sustaining a desire to see his family again and to play the piano again. Even under the most difficult conditions a clear life purpose can keep you well – or alive when others are dying.

If you are having trouble deciding on some purpose for your life, relax about it and borrow the Dalai Lama's philosophy – to be happy and useful – until your own becomes clear.

10

do you listen as well as you hear?

'You ain't learnin' nothin' while you're talkin'!' I heard this said once, and the truth of it struck a chord somewhere deep in my body.

We spend years at school being taught all about words and spelling and grammar and how to speak – yet when are we taught to listen? About one per cent of the population (and I'm being generous!) actually listen and really hear what someone else is trying to say to them. Listening is one of the most powerful tools of communication available to us. Remember the old saying: God gave us two ears and one mouth – he was hinting!

There are always two levels to any communication: the obvious one and the hidden one that we usually miss. Non-verbal communication is 80–93 per cent of everything we communicate, and it's not just body language. The actual words only account for seven per cent of the message we want to send to someone else, yet most of our training relates to the use of words.

Non-verbal messages come out in our voice tones, micro-muscle and micro-colour changes in our face, vocal variety, gestures, twitches and breathing. Most of the time we don't even know we are transmitting or receiving these messages – think about those times you have walked into an area and no one has said a word, but you know something is wrong. And you ask them, 'What's wrong?' and they say, 'Nothing!' At which point you know that there is something major wrong! And the way they said 'Nothing' is the clue – it wasn't what they said, it was *how* they said it.

At Christmas time, I was driving to Brisbane and listening to Stephen Covey's tapes, *The Seven Habits Of Highly Effective People*. His fifth principle is 'seek first to understand, then be understood'. Imagine what life would be like if everyone practised this habit. Wouldn't it be bliss!

No more interrupting; people would wait till you had finished your sentence; they would understand how you are feeling before they jumped in to give you their wisdom. Most people think they are listening when in fact they listen to 10 seconds of what you have to say, then they hold their breath with the answer poised, listening only for a gap in your conversation so they can launch into what they want to say!

How many times have we been guilty of only listening for the pause (our opportunity to speak) in the conversation, rather than intently listening to the real message behind what the person is saying?

The other Covey phrase that I thought was wonderful, and that has turned my listening skills around, is 'listen with your eyes for feelings'. Isn't that great? Listen with your eyes for feelings. In other words, when someone else is speaking, really pay attention to the way they are saying the words – look for the feelings behind what they are saying. You'll be amazed at the difference in the quality of your communication once you start to incorporate this philosophy into daily life. Especially if you also respond to those feelings.

When your attention is focused on the person with whom you are interacting, they pick it up at a non-verbal level – they know you are really interested in what they are saying. It's a great compliment (not to mention skill) to be able to tune into someone and actually identify the feelings they may be experiencing.

Of course, to do that, we have to set aside our own internal dialogue (self-talk and voices inside our heads) that say, 'Oh, I know what they need to hear,' at which point we stop listening to the feelings and words, and start waiting for a pause, so we can start talking.

Having heard or guessed the sort of feelings the other person may be experiencing, the next step is to feed back into the conversation some way of showing them you understand how they feel. Women are, generally speaking, more skilled at this behaviour than men. Women are used to responding in an animated way (their faces move and they make sympathetic noises when they listen) and this is a powerful non-verbal way of transmitting our understanding of the other person's feelings.

Comments like, 'You must have felt awful,' or, 'What a great feeling!' or, 'I would have felt upset as well,' or, 'No wonder you were angry!' indicate that you understand. You may not agree with the sentiment but you understand how they could have felt that way. It's a great way to build rapport.

So, if you want to dramatically improve your communication skills, and avoid conflict, misunderstandings and arguments, decide to practise your listening skills. Turn off your internal dialogue (you'll always think of something to say when you need to); focus on the other person; seek first to understand, then to be understood; listen with your eyes for feelings; and then feed those feelings back into the conversation, non-verbally and verbally. You'll be amazed at the differences you see and experience.

11

collages of life

How many times have you watched a group of Japanese tourists and marvelled at the number of cameras they carry and how many photos they take – of everything? And then joked about it. How many times have you groaned at a friend who always brings a camera along?

I started thinking about cameras and photographs during these holidays because my Christmas was one of the best I've ever had. My whole family was together for the first time in ten years, with all their varied assortment of children. Consequently I went mad with my camera. In fact everyone went mad with their cameras! As a result we have a fabulous array of memories in action.

Suddenly, everyone was gone. Back to various countries and states – but they left the photos with me. The place was very quiet and to ease the stab of sadness I felt, I spent ages looking through the photos. I decided to surprise each member of my family with a 'Christmas 1996 memory book'. As I write I am in the process of preparing five separate books (one for each family) documenting the events of our time together and illustrating the saga with wonderfully funny or just plain heart-melting shots of those moments. Even though it was 1996, I still remember it vividly!

Once upon a time, keen family photographers were soundly abused because they would line the troops up and then take 20 minutes to focus the camera, which needed a crane to support the long and very expensive lens. Meanwhile everyone was groaning and the smiles had become fixed into a hideous sneer. No wonder we were reluctant to take photos!

Thankfully, technology has created 'point-and-press' cameras that are within the income of most households. It's very difficult to take anything out of focus. (Although I still seem quite capable of taking a close-up of half of someone's face, particularly with my new 'super-duper focus-up-close-if-you-want' camera. But even less than perfect shots play a significant role in the memory book. They form a statement on the alcoholic status of the photographer!)

The other great technological leap is that these point-and-press cameras are becoming smaller and smaller. It's easy to pop one in your pocket or handbag and carry it with you most of the time. If mobile phones can become a form of appendage then so can a camera!

Please consider (as the car manufacturer said) capturing more of your great, fun or even apparently ordinary life moments on film. Life flashes by so quickly these days that half our life is forgotten.

Take your camera to dinner with friends, not just to birth-day parties; to the beach; on picnics; to work. Have it somewhere handy at home so when the cat or dog are in play mode you catch them; or record the night your second baby rolled over (the first one you would have taken an album's worth of photos of on this night!); or capture your garden when it looks its best. Your new car, the new dress or just a family photo of the togetherness displayed as five children sit and 'play together' (i.e. oblivious to each other's presence and eyes rigidly fixed on Gameboys!)

And once you have a collection, do something with them other than chuck them into the drawer where you have thrown all the photos of the last ten years so they now form a big, messy jumble! The task of sorting them out becomes more daunting each year.

Why not put them immediately into a collage in one of those

big perspex frames and hang it on the wall? This way your memories are always there for you to smile at, rather than being shoved away into an album you pull out on twenty-firsts or weddings!

Or do what my friends Gail and Simon do. They have five children. Gail always orders double prints and has an album for each child and one for her and Simon. She puts the relevant photos of each child into their personal album and keeps a 'central register' in theirs! What a great idea. When she finishes one album she starts another. Storage is their main problem because they do carry a camera most places, but what a fantastic gift for their children.

I know the pain of sorting out that drawer full of negatives and jumbled eras of photos – but it's worth it. Start with your recent holiday snaps and set aside some time to tackle the drawer. Buy your albums or frames first, have some Blue Tak handy to keep your memories in place on the board (or, trust me, one day you will walk in and find past boyfriends and girlfriends have slid down and mingled with your dogs and children!), and a pair of scissors to cut the shots to size and you're ready.

Perhaps you could have a wall of family history – line the walls of the hall or family room with 'this is our life' in pictorial form!

'What about videos?' I hear you cry. Videos are great and we took plenty of those as well. But you can't walk past a video so easily and feel that surge of love or laughter as you are instantly transported back to a magic moment or to that wonderful person or time. So bring out your cameras, carry them everywhere and have fun as you create collages of your life.

12

youth, part 2

Several years ago I turned the big 40. I can hear the astonished gasps out there amongst my loyal readers.

Anyway, I had a great time at my party and received many wonderful cards – one of which prompted me to write this article. On the front of the card it said, 'Turning 40? Don't think of it as middle age', and when you opened the card it said, 'Think of it as YOUTH, PART 2!'

What a great concept! On my walk this morning, I decided I was barely halfway through my life – I am going to live until 95 at least. And I'm going to be mentally alert, really fit and have a great body! (Like my 85-year-old friend, Blanch). At 55, I'm off to circuit training so I can build up strength and tone in my muscles – new research shows that muscle strength assists in living longer. I'm going to mentally exercise five times a week as well.

The old concept of physical flexibility and mental flexibility being linked to maintaining youthfulness is true. More and more studies are demonstrating the beneficial effects of both mental *and* physical training for everyone and especially for oldies – you know, the 40s and up, like me!

Recently, I was listening to an audio tape from a programme designed to improve communication skills. Halfway through, the speaker asked questions that are 'brain teasers' from Mensa, the organisation for really smart people. It was initially very depressing. I couldn't even understand the question, let alone answer it!

Yet after the first 30 or 40 questions I started to get the hang of it. A couple of questions were even easy! The purpose of doing this on the tape was to demonstrate how we can train our brains to think in different ways; or to view issues from a different perspective; to be more creative, to stay interesting and alert in general.

How we think has an enormous impact on the way we live our lives and on our physical status. In 1979, a study conducted by professor Ellen Langer at Harvard in America gathered a number of 75-year-old men and took them off to an isolated setting built to duplicate daily life as it existed twenty years before. Magazines and radio programmes were from 1959; they could only discuss issues, politics and celebrities from that era. Each person was encouraged to focus on how he thought, looked, talked and acted when he was twenty years younger.

The study group had to speak in present tense as if 1959 were today and references to family, friends and jobs could not go beyond that year. They were introduced to each other with twenty-year-old photos.

The control group talked about the events of 1959 but used past tense instead of present; 1979 music was played; magazines covered contemporary topics and films were the then current releases.

Measurements of aging were taken and the findings were as follows: in the study group (i.e. those living as if it was 1959) memory and manual dexterity improved; they were more active and self-sufficient; they looked younger, fingers actually lengthened and became more flexible; they had a stronger grip; they sat taller in their chairs. Professor Langer suggests there are a number of reasons behind these changes. One is that not seeing others grow old seems to prevent us growing old. And giving people more control over their lives keeps them behaving in more youthful ways. In other words, how we think seems to have a dramatic impact on the aging of our bodies and minds.

I used to think the phrase, 'life begins at 40', was invented by desperates who had gone over the hill! But as I reflect on what I am like now, compared with twenty years ago, I'm in much better shape than I was when I was in Youth, Part 1. I may not look quite as young as I did then, but my brain is different. I'm a little wiser (not much!) and I have a different perspective on things. I'm more self-assured, more confident in my career and know better what I want out of life. Well, for today anyway.

I've had more experiences and am becoming more accepting of me – and knowing who 'me' is. I'm better at understanding my needs; more adept at expressing them and learning how to share my feelings.

A couple of weeks ago I went out to a movie with a friend of mine and as we were walking down the street I yelled, 'Race you to the end of the street!' We took off, and laughed hysterically as we chased each other 200 metres. OK, 15 metres then.

Gee, it was fun. And immature, no doubt some of you are thinking. I realised afterwards how lucky I was to find another person my age who still thinks 'young' and had not yet grown too 'mature' to play and do silly things. You should have seen the 'old fuddy-duddies of 16 and 17' shaking their heads in pity at us!

So, what about you? Do you think young? Do you see yourself as old and mature? Do you play enough in your life? Do you do the things that were great fun for you in Youth, Part 1? Do you tell yourself you should be mature and a fuddy-duddy? Must you maintain a serious and sober outlook on life? Is it OK to go and play in the rain? Run or skip down the street? Laugh out loud in public, by and at yourself? Be overtly silly – in front of others? Are you 40 plus and in middle age? Or are you in Youth, Part 2 – and preparing yourself for Youth, Part 3? I'm not growing up yet – I'm wiser, I'm more mature, but I'm not growing up!

13

it's worth doing badly at first

Do you recall the number of times you have heard the saying, 'If it's worth doing, it's worth doing well'? Somewhere, in this age of speed, we have changed the meaning of this little cliché and most of us think if we can't do it well instantly we won't even bother trying.

How many times has that thought or attitude stopped us from learning a new skill or task, or from taking a sensible risk that could lead us to growing or developing as a person?

What about replacing this thought with, 'If it's worth doing, it's worth doing badly at first!' As children learning to walk, did we admonish ourselves for constantly falling over? Did we give up after three days because it was 'too hard' and 'we looked stupid'? Of course not – we didn't even think about how we looked. We just focused on our task, and what's more, we enjoyed the experience and loved each time we did it well.

Encouragement along the way had a lot to do with it – remember how we applaud and demonstrate our delight when our baby takes its first step? The baby thinks, 'This is great! Whatever I did, I'd better do it again the same way!' Eventually, 'practice makes perfect' (another cliché we seem to forget when judging our adult performance) and we absorb the skill of walking into our neurology and move on to the next challenge.

As adults, do we give each other encouragement for attempting new tasks, skills or behaviours? Not much. We are usually too busy judging the performance of others the same way we judge our own and we assume everyone else is judging us in the same way. Guess what! Most people are so busy thinking about themselves, they actually don't have much time to think about you and your performance!

Perhaps we need to reflect on, or review, our attitude to attempting new behaviours and experiences. What if we believed that 'if it's worth doing, it's OK to do it badly at first'? If we gave ourselves and others permission to practise until perfect (or close) and didn't expect ourselves and others to learn instantly?

In sport, we seem to be (relatively) patient with ourselves; we acknowledge we need lessons and that we need to practice. So we make time for that practice and often put our poor performance down to the lack of it, rather than to a failing in our personality, a stupid brain, the weather, stress, other people or some innate defect.

But when it comes to new behaviours or new ways of thinking, we expect instant results. We don't acknowledge the need for, let alone allocate time for, practice. We don't look for coaches or mentors or models, for people who could demonstrate how to do the new behaviour/thinking/skill, or train us or take us under their wing or guide us. Just as we look for specific coaches or trainers to learn new sports techniques, it may help us to find someone who can teach us new ways of thinking or new behaviours.

For example, if you would like to think more positively, find positive people, hang around them and ask them if they would help you by explaining how they respond or react to different situations. Then practise doing it like they do. Eventually, you'll have the basic skill which you could then develop into your own style.

The most powerful way humans learn is by modelling or copying others. Children learn most of what they ever learn by watching their parents. (This makes most parents very nervous!) Never worry that your children don't listen to you; worry that they are always watching you! So watch others; copy their behaviours and ways of thinking, and soon you will have the same level of skill they have – then you can improve on it.

Give yourself (and others) permission to have a learning phase. Make sure you learn from your mistakes; if what you are doing isn't working, see if you can work out why and then do something different. Even if you can't work out why, do something different!

Reward yourself and others for trying. Avoid punishment – it doesn't work with children and it usually doesn't work with adults. Acknowledging the effort we and others put in – not to mention the courage involved in repeatedly trying – gives us motivation to continue.

Allow yourself to be excited when you succeed – and define success in stages. Celebrate when you hit different levels of success – and blow out when you hit your target of 100 per cent successful as you defined it at the start of the process.

Let's try thinking like the little boy who, when asked if he could play tennis, replied:

'I can't hit the ball yet, but I'm good at tennis!'

14

energy-suckers

How many times have you woken up in the morning and felt great, or at least good? Well, what about had some energy? And you go out into the world and encounter someone. After five minutes with this person, you walk away with drooping shoulders, feeling depressed, muttering, 'Geez, I feel drained'.

These people are energy-suckers and are dangerous for our health! If you are married to one, seek a divorce! I'm serious – you'll live longer. (Well, OK, I say that a bit tongue-in-cheek. If you are with a recovering energy-sucker, then give them a second chance!)

Recently, The Seminar Company promoted a tour of Australia and New Zealand with John Gray and Wayne Dyer and me. People kept rushing up to John Gray claiming, 'You saved my marriage, thank you' and up to Wayne Dyer thanking him for 'saving my life'. About six rushed up to me and said, 'I divorced my energy-sucker after I heard you speak'! And I still felt I had made a contribution. I knew they would live longer – and be happier!

Energy-suckers are typically cynics and pessimists. Cynics pride themselves on not 'having anyone pull the wool over my eyes' or 'not being a gullible idiot'. There is a place for being sensible and going into things with your eyes open, but not to be suspicious of everything until proven squeaky clean and good for you. If you choose to live life that way, then keep it to yourself – don't infect everyone you meet with your particular brand of misery.

Looking at the world and expecting to see the bad in people

usually acts like a self-fulfilling prophecy. Look for the worst and you will find it – people will never disappoint you.

It's also important to notice what you put your attention on. If you are driving in the car and someone says to you, 'Gosh, there's a lot of pink cars around at the moment', you say, 'Are there?' because you have not seen any. Of course, from the moment that person highlights the pink cars for you, you see them everywhere! They didn't suddenly appear from nowhere – they were always there but you hadn't noticed them; your attention was elsewhere. We notice what we focus our attention on.

So, is your attention on the negative? Are you 'naturally' pessimistic? Pessimistic people often describe themselves as 'realistic'. They're not really – they do expect the worst, and so their attention is on the worst, and consequently it does become their reality. No one is naturally pessimistic – it's a habit we learn, from our parents or from significant others in our lives.

So break the habit! Become an energy-giver. To have successful relationships – personally and professionally – we need to give energy. We also need to fill up our own energy tanks so we have reserves to give to others.

How many of us walk around being kind and caring and concerned and witty and charming and friendly and patient and tolerant to relative strangers all day long, only to come home at night to the people who would lie down in front of a truck for us, and growl 'leave me alone'?

Spot the problem! We can't expect our loved ones to continue to put up with this sort of behaviour on a regular basis – why should they? They have been looking forward to us coming home, they are full of energy, waiting to see us, and we walk in the door and destroy all their enthusiasm!

Make a conscious effort to become an energy-giver at home – unwind before you arrive home; take a few deep breaths before you greet the family; do something that recharges your energy battery so you have reserves to give.

Think of five things that make you feel good – dancing, singing, laughing, sleeping, reading, fishing, building, having a massage, visiting friends, shopping, playing sport, writing, gardening, swimming, lying on the beach, looking at a beautiful scene, being silent – there are millions of alternatives from which you can choose. Then do them regularly.

Of course, for some people, this is not an easy task. If I asked you to list 50 things that made you feel awful, it would be an easy task. Some could go way past 50! But to focus on things that boost your energy, make you feel great and make you feel alive – not so easy.

Put your attention on those things (and how often you do them) that make you feel energised; and then place it on people or things that are energy-suckers in your life. Eliminate the sucking – accentuate the giving! Seek other energy-givers – people who leave you feeling recharged and revitalised. Hang around them a lot.

If you have energy-suckers at work – beware! They drag the whole culture down – it only takes one energy-sucker to deflate a community of people. Be very selective about the people you employ. Spot the energy-sucker before they attach themselves to your lifeline.

If you are identifying with being cynical or pessimistic, then work out what happened to you to make you take up this habit. And then work out how to change the habit. Make the effort and you'll be amazed at how much happier you and the people around you are.

Sometimes, in a stressful period, we can change from being an energy-giver to a sucker. That's OK, except it makes our condition worse because everyone around us soon tires of being drained and they start to avoid us. So energy-sucking can be triggered by a temporary period of great stress – but rather than suck another person's energy, why not do more things for yourself to boost your own reserves? Particularly when you believe you have *no* time for yourself to 'indulge' yourself with luxuries like a massage or a trip to a comedy movie. This is exactly the time you owe it to yourself and to those around you to do what I consider essential – taking responsibility for your own needs. Go to it, champ – and become a positively radiant light bulb because you have so much energy to give!

15

frogs and change

Remember that story of the two frogs? The frog that is put into the saucepan of boiling water jumps straight out, while the one that goes into the cold water, and is slowly brought to the boil, dies. Now for those animal lovers out there who are shocked and appalled by this concept, let me rush to say I don't know if they used real frogs.

That story started me thinking about us and our similarity to frogs! So many people slowly subside into the seething mass of mediocrity, which in normal language means how easy it is for us not to notice a continuous, slow decline in the quality of our lifestyles.

Think of the last time a crisis occurred in your life – something that precipitated a sudden and dramatic change. Although it was terrible at the time I bet it made you rethink life, your goals, hopes, dreams, purpose and the meaning of your life in a big way. Just like being dropped into a vat of boiling water – you'll make a very quick choice and change.

So should we look at something that forces change on us as bad? Or could we maybe look at a bigger picture – if we played a game and you had to pretend you were looking back on this sudden change time from the future, what growth and development did the incident spur in you? Did it change the direction of your life? Or trigger you to do something that you had wanted to do for years, but hadn't had the courage, impetus or time to do?

If we want to make changes in our lives we usually think about making one change at a time, and doing it gradually so it's not too stressful or scary. There is some merit to this concept, of course. But maybe there's also merit in the idea of throwing ourselves into 'boiling water' and making lots of changes at once.

It's more frightening, more challenging and probably more stressful, but you might surprise yourself by your resourcefulness and abilities. Often, it takes extreme circumstances to bring out qualities you never knew you had.

Difficult situations also help you develop confidence in your feelings or intuition or 'inner knowing'.

Sometimes we are working in a job, for example, that we feel is wrong but we don't have the courage to 'take the plunge' and do what we feel is right – even if we don't have another job lined up. A friend of mine has just left her full-time paying job at which she was very successful. She knew it wasn't what she really wanted to do, so she decided she would take responsibility for herself – she left.

She didn't just leave and wander aimlessly, wondering what she should do. She researched and made phone calls and networked and she had some cash reserves to keep her going. Now she is 'between jobs' and feeling great when we (and she!) thought it would be stressful and scary. She is actively searching for her niche, and is excited about life like she hasn't been for years.

A divorce is a good example of the 'boiling water' syndrome. At the time our whole world is shattered. Yet, ask most divorced people five years after the divorce how life is different, and the answers are similar. 'It was awful at the time but it's the best thing that ever happened to me. Since then I've . . .'

Or deaths. I had the great fortune to travel around Australia recently with Sara Henderson, who is a really amazing person. Here is another example of being thrown into boiling water – Sara's husband died and left her with a million dollars of debt. (Can't get much more boiling than that!) Since then, she has become a famous author, wise investor, international speaker and generally has learned more skills than you can poke a stick at!

Sometimes, it's exhilarating to be thrown into boiling water! See it as an opportunity for you to test yourself and your abilities, to see how good you really are – and that's usually much better than you ever thought.

16

a real holiday?

Recently, I had the good fortune to visit Canada for a holiday. After a week's recovery, my brain started firing again.

How long is it since you had a holiday? A real one – not just time off work. A time where you weren't looking after a family member; or spending obligatory time with the 'family'; or travelling with a difficult partner so you combined time away with heartbreak; or travelling alone and feeling desperately lonely; or using your holiday time to renovate the house, paint, fix the car, and so on.

It dawned on me over there that it was 10 years since I had a wonderful, relaxing, no responsibility, emotionally comfortable, interesting break. This time, no one could phone me or fax me or reach me; my most challenging decision was where to have breakfast, lunch and dinner. I have had only one other holiday with no phone and I recognised then the impact a telephone has on our daily lives. When I came home from that holiday, it was amazing the way the noise of the telephone ring made me jump.

Only then did I realise that although the telephone is a great addition to our lives it also takes its toll. I think we must all be (subconsciously) just that little bit alert and tense, ready to jump at the handset as soon as it jangles! Mobile phones and pagers now make this far more constant.

Have you ever had an experience where you become so absorbed in an activity that the memory of the phone, and therefore the tension, slowly fades and you relax completely? At that moment, the phone gremlin, who has been waiting patiently, makes the phone jangle its loudest ring and you jump five feet and out of your skin? That's the sort of impact phones can have on us.

So beware – and don't take your mobile on holiday with you unless you keep it hidden until you want to ring out. For maximum relaxation value in our rushed, urgent, do it now, expect it yesterday society, go on a holiday where you have *no* access to phones. Even if the thought scares you. I promise you'll make it to the end of the best holiday you've ever had!

In Canada, I didn't have to do anything in a hurry; or do anything I didn't want to; and I could have as much fun as I liked. I had new experiences like playing in a snowstorm and riding in gondolas millions of miles (or so it seemed) above the ground. I discovered a fantastic Canadian beer called Shaftsbury Honey Ale. In other words, I had a great break. And my body and mind loved it. My creativity has since soared – where I was stuck before the break, the ideas and thoughts ran freely afterwards. My friends say I'm speaking more slowly and sound and look more relaxed. OK, lets be honest, *I* even know I'm more relaxed!

How easy it is, with life's daily pressures, to forget the need for *real* holidays. Not just time off work. They don't have to be expensive trips overseas. Camping and spending time in isolated bush, forests, tropical paradises, the beach or in any of the many glorious natural settings Australia has is one of the best ways to recover, relax and restore our hearts, spirits, bodies and minds. Bushwalking is a great way to combine exercise, fresh air, magnificent scenery and the peace that comes from being surrounded by natural beauty.

In the past, if I have travelled overseas or away from home, I had been driven (not that I knew it at the time) to see, do and experience everything. Because it was there. And I had to get the best value for money! Even if I came home more exhausted than I left. Was it age or immaturity or was I just brain damaged?

Luckily, I have seen the light (or a blinding flash of the obvious) and realised that the old Buddhist saying 'less is more' holds true for holidays as well.

We seem to be such a 'more' driven society – we cram more and more into what we call 'life'. And 'more' seems to mean quality for many people. We boast or feel proud of expensive, round the world, 'every country included' tours. We feel cheated, or that we are wasting time, if we stop or go slow or spend time absorbing the energy of the place we are in.

Why walk the entire Milford Track in New Zealand in one day and nearly kill yourself with the pace, not to mention miss the spectacular scenery, so you can see the rest of New Zealand in that week you have off? Instead, you could take the three days it normally takes and you could feel the exhilaration of a unique experience; you could absorb the silence and let it penetrate and calm your soul; you could give your body gentle exercise, breathe fresh air, and you could above all slow down and rest, recover, relax. Have a real holiday at least once a year.

As one of the 'No Fear' T-shirts says, 'Everyone who lives dies; but not everyone who dies has lived.' Get a life. Have a real holiday.

career
and money

1

the nightmare of the two-career couple

Welcome to 2003, the age of equality where men are men and women have to be both. (Ha, ha, just joking, everyone!) Well, a bit anyway. However, all this new-found independence is giving women more heart attacks. Because now we are doing everything else we used to do *and* working. Life seems to be speeding up exponentially. Economic conditions and materialism mean that most couples are two-career couples. This is where the nightmare starts.

Time is the most important commodity we have. Western society lifestyles have eroded the concept of 'plenty of time', so much so that we now have to talk about 'quality time' with our children. What ever happened to lots of time with the children? Or our partners? Even if we do have time now, it's usually incredibly rushed.

My view of relationships is that two separate satellites (individuals) come together to form a relationship which is a living, breathing organism; it needs nurturing, effort, attention and care. In heterosexual relationships for example . . .

In the early phases of a heterosexual relationship, for example, both parties spend time, energy and effort establishing 'the relationship' (see diagram a). They continue to nurture, support and grow 'the relationship' for some time. Then it becomes permanent (in theory anyway). Now, we have both partners working *and* learning to live with each other, which makes the first year a bit tense. No one, of course, gives us a manual on

Diagram a.

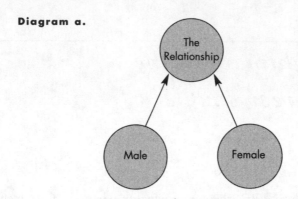

Diagram b.

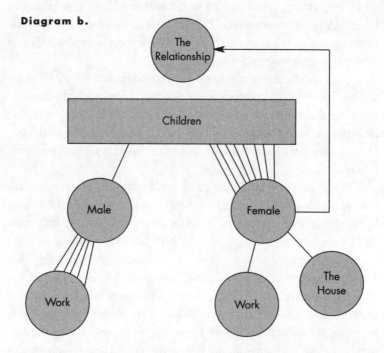

how to 'do' relationships, so we struggle through the first year. We just have to make do with the lessons we learned from watching our parents (or TV).

So now we know how to live with each other and combine hectic work and travel schedules as well as play (which includes time and energy for sex). Then we have children.

This changes the diagram dramatically! (As you read the following, remember I am generalising. There are of course exceptions to these rules so please, take no offence!)

Now, the man immediately goes into 'children, what a responsibility, I must protect, provide and perform' mode, and spends time with the children but *bulk* time at work to provide for another person, school fees, a home, food and life. He's now an adult who's totally responsible for others. He infrequently remembers that the relationship needs special attention and often gets jealous of the time the woman gives the child.

The woman becomes an instant child fanatic and devotes mega time, energy and effort towards this child/children and occasionally remembers the relationship, at which point she makes an effort to nurture it.

Then, in my opinion, the real rot sets in. The woman has to work. Or wants to work. If she cannot find part-time work she has to work full-time. Now she is torn between spending time with the children *and* on the relationship, *and* at work. Soon, she is completely riddled with guilt, exhausted and burnt out and feels she can do only so much. So she figures 'hang the relationship' because other things are more urgent and need immediate attention. (See diagram b.)

Men are much better at being what the Dalai Lama calls 'wise selfish'. Women, I believe, often become martyrs. We rarely give ourselves time out, because we feel guilty that there is all the housework to be done; we feel we don't spend enough time with the children because we are working and so we can't take even more time away from them to take care of ourselves. Men are quite happy to go and play golf or sport or go to the pub. Men become annoyed because they tell their partners that they can go and play too, but women won't, because they are worrying about quality and amount of time with the children . . . and the cost of the babysitter!

Before the knives come out and stab me, let me say I am not suggesting that we should ignore our children, but I think there needs to be some realistic evaluation of the way we are living our lives. Both partners are exhausted; neither has time to nurture the relationship and children rarely see a happy, loving, relaxed couple on which they can then model their own relationships.

The Australian Bureau of Statistics produced a survey in 1992, titled *Focus on Families: work and family responsibilities.* It basically says that women are still doing everything around the house and caring for the children *and* working and that they are stressed out. In a big way. And where we once thought that when the children left home, we could breathe a sigh of relief and have time to ourselves again, we have to rethink. Because now our aging parents require looking after.

Apart from that, imagine what happens to a couple in a relationship if they pay attention only to work and the children for 20 years. They wake up one day and realise they have been waking up every day next to the same 'stranger' for 10 years and now the only company they have at home is this 'stranger'. No wonder marriages break up once the children are gone – there *is* no relationship! What do we talk about if we don't mention children or work?

Relationships are like plants in pots. They need fertilising, feeding, watering, loving, caring and communication to grow and blossom and develop. If we ignore a potted plant for ten weeks, it dies. And it doesn't look good even if we ignore it for ten days!

Two-career couples are fraught with danger whether we have children or not. This does not mean we shouldn't both have fulfilling, rewarding careers, but please recognise the need to nurture both ourselves *and* the relationship and to make special time to do both. Working adds a new dimension of fulfilment and recognition that is really important for most people, so working has enriched our lives (if we love our work). It's just the way we work, and the way our culture has established rules for who does what in a home environment, that poses problems.

I know men are changing and taking on more responsibility at home and with children but, as Hugh McKay's book *Reinventing Australia* suggests, not much!

Start thinking about how you treat your partner and how much time and energy you spend nuturing your relationship. It's worth it!

2

an affair with work

Have you ever wondered if your partner is having an affair? Long hours; home late from work; fewer phone calls; less conversation. Signs that make you think something is wrong.

Well, they may not be having an affair with another person but they may be having an affair with their work! This idea emerged during a discussion with a female friend of mine last week. We were talking about the dynamics of her relationship with her husband. Both had been working full-time until they decided the relationship needed someone to pay attention to it; so she sold her business, and he was going to be home earlier and travel overseas less.

So, she did and he didn't! What a common story. The problem is he absolutely loves what he is doing. It challenges him, stimulates him, attracts him, and it's fun; and she feels like she is his second priority.

Many men, and (fewer) women, find work so satisfying that, although the home relationship is important, they don't pay attention to it until a crisis occurs. Until the person who is taking second place to work shouts 'enough'! Or leaves without shouting. They may not have complained because they didn't want to add more pressure to an already stressed person.

To love our work is wonderful. We spend the bulk of our lives doing whatever this work is. To persevere with something we hate every workday is to damage our minds, bodies and spirits. But there needs to be a balance.

We need to recognise how important our home life is for superior work performance. Hundreds of men have come up to me after I have spoken at a conference to say that the thing that interferes with their work performance more than anything else is conflict at home. Women comment that problems with relationships interfere with almost everything they do.

At the end of a day at work, how much energy do you have for your relationship? If you start off with 100 per cent, work for a day and come home, what percentage do you have when you arrive home?

Relationships are living, breathing 'organisms'. They are like an exotic plant you have searched for all your life. Finally you discover this unique and beautiful plant and you buy it. You put it in a perfect spot, feeling great that you finally found it. Then life continues and catches you in its swirling chaos. And three months or years later when you suddenly remember this precious plant, you rush back to see if it's OK.

Too late. Without watering, fertilising or nurturing, it has died. Now, with great sadness, you realise how little effort it would have taken to keep this plant alive and well. And you stop and reassess your priorities, and vow never to make the same mistake again.

Perhaps if we talked about issues like this more often, we could avoid some of the failed relationships that are a hallmark of today's frenetic lifestyles. We could improve communication. How important is your work? And your home relationship? Are you taking home and your partner for granted? Do you expect them to continue putting up for years with seeing you for a few hours during the week when you are stressed, tired, irritable and uncommunicative?

A man said to me last week, 'I was so busy working to provide them with a nice home and schools that I missed my children growing up.' Would they have benefited more from growing up in a 'modest' house with parents who spent time together and loved each other; or growing up in a nice house, going to a 'good' school, with parents who became strangers and then divorced?

Children are the innocent victims of an affair with work. All on the pretext of 'I did this to provide you with what I believed was best for you.' 'I did this for you' is often greeted with, 'You did it for YOU; you were never there when we needed you; you were too busy being important at work.'

Be careful of work. Enjoy it; learn from it; grow through it; gain satisfaction and pride from it; even love it – but know its place. Don't let it be an escape from a difficult situation at home. Don't let it seduce you away from your family – even if it's much easier and less complicated at work, one day you will wake up and feel empty.

Human beings need a balance – something that fulfils our hearts as well as our minds. And we need to recognise the real importance of our family and home life. I know, it's been said a million times and it's all 'ho hum' now. But it keeps happening. We must be stupid or we are forgetting to think of the consequences of our actions. So where is your priority? Your words may say family but what does your behaviour say?

Instead of seeking all your satisfaction from work, try having an ongoing affair with your partner – they kiss better than work and are much cuddlier!

3

how to want what you have

Timothy Miller has written a book called *How to Want What You Have* – isn't that a great title? I found it when doing some research on happiness and what it is and how to find it.

The title also made me start to think about what we have in our relationships and families – and how happy we are with 'our lot', as our grandparents used to say. How many families are ripped apart because we need more and more and more? Kids must have the latest (usually expensive) joggers; and the 'right' clothes ('don't be stupid, I can't wear that – it's last year's and *everyone* else will be wearing platforms'); we need a TV in every room; several phones (God forbid we should have to stay in the one place near a landline for the whole call!); at least two stereo systems; and every kitchen appliance known to personkind!

We are a dangerously materialistic society, with more 'things' than we've ever had in the past and yet we have the highest rate of unhappiness ever. What's wrong with this picture?

Maybe we need to think seriously about 'wanting what we have' – acknowledging and being grateful for everything we have. Things like our health; a loving family; great friends; sunny days; any job at all; a roof over our heads even if it's not a mansion! Maybe I sound a tad preacher-like, but I don't see us bursting with happiness and joy with all our 'things' and possessions.

In fact, we seem to become more miserable as we lust after the Porsche or the huge house, but what we often fail to notice is that those people work 18-hour days to have those 'luxuries' and generally have *no* social or home life – which might be OK for them and maybe not so OK for their families. And that sort of lifestyle may not be one that would enhance your happiness.

Perhaps we could have family rituals around the dinner table that would help us appreciate our good fortune. Every night, we might (corny as it sounds) choose to say two qualities we love about each person at the table; or two things we are grateful for in our lives, our home, our relatives or our work. Maybe it's a bit like saying grace before a meal – giving thanks for what we have in our lives. Even if it's not a gourmet, three-course meal – let's want what we have! Constantly wanting more is not the route to ongoing joy and happiness.

I was listening to a tape by Gary Smalley last week and he was discussing the importance of 'honouring' your partner, children and family. His description of honour was that whenever we thought of them, or saw them, we would gasp in awe and think, '*Wow* – they are fantastic!' Even if we didn't exactly feel like it at that second, it would be helpful to remember that this is a person we do honour!

Try it for a while – it's fun and works really well. (It helps if you both do it.) It will seem very unnatural at first (although I wonder if it wasn't natural in the first days of our love) and funny (ha ha funny) but soon may become a valuable way of communicating our love. It may even remind us on a daily basis of what we love about our partner.

Try honouring them for who they already are – not what you want them to be. And that's the crux of this article: honour what they are and who they are, just as they are. Want what we have, as opposed to spending our lives wanting them to be different people. The irony is that if we accept them for who they are and want them just as they are, it's far more likely that they will voluntarily move in the direction that you thought you wanted them to change!

Maybe we could whisper a phrase or prayer to ourselves each night thanking life, ourselves, the universe, God, or anyone or thing we like for what we already have. It's fine to want more out of life, but let's really value what we already have, rather than postponing happiness or contentment until we have 'more' ... and more! Maybe it's another step on the path to true happiness?

4

how to get what you want out of life

Did you know that less than five per cent of people have specific goals; less than three per cent actively write their goals and less than one per cent set specific deadlines to attain their goals? This was reported in the literature from The Young Presidents Organisation. Bill Bean, an author and businessman with an impressive list of credentials and business successes, quoted these figures in his course summary.

I don't know how or where he found these figures but I think the concept of goals is worth exploring further. It still astounds me that more people do not think about, let alone write down, their business, personal and life goals.

It has to be the cheapest and most effective way to move you much closer to where you want to be in life. That's if you've taken the time to think about where you would like to be!

Why do so few people think specifically about goals in their lives and fail to write them down? Perhaps it's because we don't understand how the brain works. Or perhaps we are just lazy? Or we just don't understand how effective a technique this really is?

Whatever the reason, I hope that if you are not a goal-setter already you will be one at the end of this article!

Firstly, our brain works in incredibly complex and sophisticated ways and it is wonderfully equipped to keep us on track – once we set one! Simplistically, we can think of our mind as comprising two parts – the conscious and subconscious minds.

180

Sort of like the captain of a ship and the person in the engine-room driving the ship. The captain represents the conscious mind and the engine-room person the subconscious.

As the captain is on the bridge, he can see what is happening and make decisions based on the information he has; he sends these decisions down to the engine-room person (the subconscious) who in blind faith (literally, because she or he can't see anything) carries out these orders.

In essence, it is the engine-room person who is literally running the ship with direction and guidance from the captain (conscious mind). If the captain fails to give the engine-room person any instructions, either nothing happens or the engine-room person makes any decision he or she can, based on the limited information available.

So, if you fail to think about your path in life, the direction you would like to take, the place you would like to end up, and how you would like to travel, then your 'captain' has no directions for your 'engine-room person'. Who knows where you will end up?

It's important to set goals so your subconscious mind has some purposeful direction and guidance.

I don't really believe people are lazy – I think many have never been exposed to the significance of goal-setting. Have you ever been at a seminar or conference and someone has made you write down a few goals based on what you learned? You travel home, file the notes somewhere and several years or months later you uncover the notes. And to your amazement, you achieved all those goals without specifically focusing on them?

Ah ha! That is the power of our subconscious. Once we give it a focus and target, it sets its track like a guided missile; unless we change the direction we initially encoded, it will steadily and surely make its way to the specified target.

It is extraordinarily powerful in achieving what you want, so why not try it? There's nothing like personally experiencing the benefits.

If I give you some questions that can trigger your thinking, you may choose to make a list of goals at the end of this article. In order to set these in 'subconscious concrete', you need to write them down. It's important to be as specific as you can, so your target is well identified for your subconscious – otherwise it may find a close target, but not exactly the one you wanted.

Age is never a barrier – you are never too young or old to think about and write down goals.

What do you want to be doing at work in the next year? At the end of five years? At the end of ten years? When you retire?

What do you want your home life to be like now? In one year? In five years? In ten years? When you retire?

What sort of relationships do you want in your life now? In one year? In five years and in ten years?

What hobbies would you like to develop? Or what new skills would you like to learn? By when? (For example, tennis, photography, painting, dancing, playing a musical instrument, scuba diving, writing novels, sport, fitness.)

What are activities that recharge your life batteries? Do you do them often enough? If not, how often would you like to be doing them? (Realistically! You can't have a massage every day – yet!)

What new business, communication, listening or relationships skills would you like to enhance in the next one, two, five, seven or twelve months?

What fun activities would you like to have in your life? How often?

What holiday would you like to have this year? And for the next few years?

These are just some of the areas in which you could set goals. The more specific you are, the more likely you are to achieve exactly what you want. Remember you can constantly upgrade your written descriptions as you change, or as your life changes.

Go on – be in the one per cent that maximise their potential and get what they want. Or at least have a chance of getting it. Buy a 'goal book' to track your success. Enjoy!

5

how to be wealthy

Recently there was an article in *The Bulletin* on Paul Clitheroe, the 'money man'. I had the good fortune to meet Paul years ago at a conference and was enchanted by him as a person and by the wonderful way he made money matters sound simple, easy and interesting.

Obviously, many others have found the same thing! One line he is quoted as saying was in response to the question, 'How do I get rich?' His answer was, 'Spend less than you earn.' Now, that is a wellness comment if ever I heard one! A blinding flash of the obvious that almost everyone ignores.

Of course, we sigh, as if we know that; but if we all know it, then why don't more of us follow this simple and effective rule?

I started to think about financial wellness and, although I have no qualifications or expertise in this area, I did start my career as a physiotherapist and we were not paid well. I also started life as the child of an only parent who struggled very hard to earn enough to support three children. And I am now in a position of what I consider to be financial security, so I've been there and done that! And I recognise that financial worries are often the biggest causes of stress.

When I explored some of the strategies I used along the way, not only did I discover that Paul was right but I remembered some ideas that may be useful to others.

Firstly, have you ever taken time to write down absolutely

everything you spend each day for a month? And compared it with what you earn? It's a very interesting exercise which does take time but it's well worth it. How many times have you said, 'I don't know where the money goes. It just seems to disappear'?

Be rigid about noting every cent that goes out (the cents add up very quickly!) whether it's on lunch and other meals, take-away foods, a bridge toll, transport fares, magazines, rent, clothes, presents, cigarettes, sweets, car expenses, coffees and other daily 'needs'. Then there's regular or one-off payments like insurances or payments on the car, TV, computer or other items on hire purchase, lay-by, lease and so on. Not to mention credit card payments.

Once you have been through this often enlightening (and sometimes terrifying) experience, you can compare what you spend each month with what you earn. If what you earn is less than what you spend, you are in deep doo doo, to use a very technical financial term.

Then look at where you can save money – like make your own lunches; cook at home using more vegetables and fruits instead of lots of meat; buy less takeaway food; ask yourself, 'Do I need that extra shirt/dress/outfit?'; are there cheaper ways of travelling – like walking (which is better for you as well as being cheaper); look at every area and ask yourself if you can make changes.

Just as important as becoming aware of what you really do spend is your attitude to saving (or becoming rich!). Are you really committed to saving money and are you prepared to be disciplined about it? Or will you constantly give in to temptation – like a binge dieter? Because it seems to me that by being consistent and disciplined with myself I saved enough for a deposit on my first unit from a very meagre salary. And lots of people on low salaries seem to be able to save using this thinking.

This doesn't mean you deny yourself everything of value. I think celebration is critical for the success of any venture in which you are attempting to change behaviour. So plan when you are going to lash out – set a goal or a target that when you have saved 'x' amount you will celebrate in a way that doesn't mean you spend every cent you just saved!

Anyway, if we want to stop worrying and stressing about money, we have to do something to take charge of our financial situation. This is just the first step. At least know exactly what is happening to your money and where it goes and then think about your beliefs about saving – and being rich.

Then we can start exploring courses on learning about money and investment; watching programmes like Paul Clitheroe's; reading books on the subject; finding a financial mentor; seeing a financial planner; setting goals for saving – just to name a few ideas. Start right now – grab a piece of paper and make your list of what you have spent so far today. Who knows, this may be the first day on your path to becoming a millionaire!

6

money and wellness

I don't know who originally said this but it's profound. Most people spend the first forty years of their lives ignoring their health to make money. Then they spend the last forty years spending that money to regain their health. How true. And how stupid!

Ellen Kreidman, American author of *Light His Fire*, writes of the early days of her marriage where they were young and poor as churchmice; their dream was to go on an exotic cruise and she convinced him that if they didn't do it now, they would be in their sixties before they had another chance.

While on board, they met an elderly couple who were very wealthy – the older woman was covered in expensive jewellery and looked well. However, as they talked she gave Ellen the news that she was dying. She and her rich husband had delayed having time together or going on holidays in order to make money. Finally, they had the money to relax. But not the life. When they found out she had only months to live, their whole perspective on life changed.

Why wait for a life-threatening crisis to put our attitude to wellness, life and money in perspective? Most people assume we all work just to earn money. Wrong! Some do, of course, but the majority of people work because it's their main source of meeting people; they get recognition and a sense of achievement and satisfaction from their work; it educates them; gives them new experiences; it gives them a sense of purpose and meaning; and . . . it gives them money.

If we're smart we'll find a job we love that does give us some of those qualities. If we are working and we hate every day we are there, we are on our way to some form of illness. We need to change quickly or learn to love something about that job.

For those of you who stay at your jobs for most of your waking hours – ask yourself, 'Why?' Are you doing this to avoid problems at home? Are you overcommitted? Are you obsessed with success, earning more and having security? Or are you trapped on the treadmill and in the habit of ignoring the rest of your life, not to mention your family? Is this the way you want to end up – rich, tired and lonely? Or worse, rich, alone and sick?

How can we make sure we have a life, as well as earn money? Either decide to change your attitude now, or wait to develop cancer, have the heart attack or other major illness, or a divorce – which are the most common triggers for life re-evaluation.

There is no magic answer and we know it – the change has to be one that we make a commitment to because we see or feel or become aware that our health is gradually being eroded; or that we hardly ever laugh any more; or that our partner and children don't talk to us any more because we are never there; or that we never see friends because we (and they) are too busy working? We need to think about what we are giving up to make all this money.

I wonder if money does buy all the things we think it will. A phrase I heard some time ago has stuck with me: 'I've been rich and happy and poor and happy. If I had a choice, I'd rather be rich and happy!' Of course we all would, but bulk money isn't a prerequisite for happiness. And a lust for money destroys happiness.

Money usually doesn't make loneliness disappear; it doesn't boost our immune system; it doesn't make us feel fulfilled; it doesn't give us a sense of community or purpose.

It doesn't replace loved ones and it doesn't make or break

relationships – but our attitude to money does. If we expect money to cure all our problems, to give us the car that will make us happy or the house that will make us happy or the clothes, people, TVs, stereos, and other material possessions that will surely add excitement to our lives, our attitude needs work.

Money is good to have, security is essential, but life, love, family, friends and wellness are far more important (which we realise when we don't have them) – and they are things that all the money you are earning while you are missing life cannot buy.

7

rich vs wealthy

Would you rather die rich or wealthy? This question popped into my mind following a discussion with a great lover of life – Lisa. She said she had been wealthy for some of her life but rich for all of it.

What a fantastic way of viewing life, because when you think about it we are all rich – fabulously rich. Some of us are wealthy – which doesn't necessarily lead to a rich life.

I have just finished a phone call to a friend of mine who enriches my life more than I can say. Jan is the most outrageous person who always has me in stitches when I speak to her, in person or on the phone. I love having her in my life; our friendship is a jewel much more precious than inanimate, cold, albeit sparkling diamonds!

What does a rich life mean to you and your family? Is it the love and compassion and sharing and caring that being a family (whether it's a family of friends or your blood relatives) brings? Or the number of different experiences you have in life? Or is it to be well and bursting with vitality? Or perhaps contentment with what we have? Is it to be involved with your community, helping others? Perhaps to have a balance between all areas in your life?

What would make a life fulfilling and rewarding and satisfying? Answering these questions helps you understand the components of a rich life – for you.

How would you define a 'rich' person? Someone who laughs

a lot? Someone who enjoys every moment? Someone who knows themselves and is true to their values, beliefs and morals? A person who loves learning and seeks new opportunities whenever they can? Someone who makes the most of all aspects of their lives?

Like my very special friend, Mela. Full of energy and enthusiasm, she has always tackled her life with gusto. She had a wonderful single life; completed a degree at University; started her own business; married her dream man (who is gorgeous with a capital G!); lived overseas; had two beautiful girls; went back to study art after the children were born; adored learning to sculpt and has just had her first successful exhibition. Whew! And she's only halfway through her life!

Before anyone mumbles, 'It's OK for her, she must be loaded' – no, she's not! And she has had some terrible sadness in her life, but she always experienced it, learned from it and moved on. Her lust for life (passion is too tame for Mela!) makes her the richest person I know.

A lust for life doesn't have to cost a fortune. And a rich life can be a very simple one. Someone who has the ability to enjoy every moment of their day is truly rich. Even the relatively unpleasant moments. Look at how a toddler lives life. We are all born rich – we lose the knack along the way. Do you wake up, go for a walk and feel humbled by the beauty that exists around you? Really look at the trees and sky and clouds; notice the birds and their songs; see other people enjoying themselves (sometimes you have to look for a while!) – make as many magic moments as you can.

Revel in the glory that you are alive! And make sure you make the most of being alive – lots of people die at 30 but their bodies keep walking around. Before anyone 'bah humbugs' me and says 'She obviously wrote this while on drugs!', anyone who knows me will tell you that I'm really like this – most of the time anyway. I try to make the most of life's experiences.

I always expect highs and am bursting with enthusiasm when

they occur and really experience to the fullest extent the lows. But that's part of the richness, isn't it? To be able to feel. Most of us die without having allowed our real feelings and emotions to surface since the age of two. No matter how wealthy you are, if you can't feel both elation and sadness and the levels in between, you are poor.

If you have friends and environments that allow you to be yourself, you are rich beyond your wildest dreams. Having that unconditional acceptance is a rare quality we need to actively seek in our lives if it is absent.

If you have one person that loves you for you or even a pet who enthusiastically greets you when you arrive home, you are rich.

If you have a job at all, you are rich! If you have a job you love and put great energy and enthusiasm into, you are hugely rich! Even if you have a job you don't particularly enjoy, be grateful you have one and put your best into it – you will be amazed at how much more job satisfaction you experience. You may even be noticed and promoted to another job you love.

We are all rich – some of us just don't notice it as much. Some of us choose to focus on aspects of material poverty – stop it! Seek instead those areas I have outlined and the many more you may discuss, and focus on those. Develop a lust for life – a love of *your* life and a passion for what you have and you'll burst with richness!

8

he or she who dies with the most points . . . still dies

There is a story about Adam and Eve in the Garden of Eden. Adam and Eve have been on earth for some time and are surrounded by family members. For centuries they have all been living happily, playing games and having fun in a community atmosphere. One day, bored with just playing games, one of the team suggested they score points for various aspects of the games they played.

So they did. And suddenly, competition, rivalry and aggression were born. The family members started fighting and scheming to win the most points – because the person who died with the most points won!

The moral of this story is – won what? What did the points mean? What was the purpose of winning? Let alone point-scoring!

I recently bought a 'No Fear' T-shirt that I now use in seminars and across the front, in big bold letters are the words, 'He or she who dies with the most points . . . still dies!' Ain't it the truth! I wonder what we really value. It seems that most people are focused on winning maximum points, dollars, houses, cars, etc. before they die – to the detriment of their wellness and happiness.

How many people do you know who seem obsessed with winning these nebulous 'points'? And they're usually miserable! 'Points' don't matter – fulfilment matters; happiness matters; contributing matters; growing and developing matters; sharing and loving matters; family and friends matter; having fun matters.

It's essential to have a purpose in life – one that has some altruistic aspects to it and is not just materially driven! But what is the value of being so focused on a goal like winning the most points that all other aspects of life are excluded? Does winning that many 'points' really matter? What areas in your life really give you fulfilment? Are you really satisfied by just scoring 'points' and beating others? Beating them to what? Early death?

How many people tread all over others, in the search for more points? They ignore their feelings, and those of others, and the emotional side of life. They end up having mid-life crises, because they realise how little time they have left and how unhappy they really are. And what schmucks they have been!

There's another, more humorous aspect to scoring points. John Gray in his book *Men are from Mars, Women are from Venus* says that in relationships men and women have different point-scoring strategies!

He suggests men casually stroll through life and when the woman does something wrong, he scores 100 (for example) points against her. These are quickly removed by her doing something to rectify the situation.

On the other hand, women score small numbers of points against men much more often – for minor 'misdemeanours'. And we bottle them up, and up and up until one day we hit the threshold (another arbitrary figure!) and then BOY, does he get it! And we women don't just quote the latest 'straw that broke the camel's back'. We cite, in tremendous detail, every incident from the last three months for which we scored points. We remember words, voice intonations and looks!

That is just another example of point-scoring not always working. It's much better to talk about issues along the way – and fellas, don't accuse us of nagging. Constant communication is much better than the almighty blast we save up!

So, dear readers, do you score points in your life? Is that

really what drives you? Are there alternative ways for you to search for fulfilment and happiness, other than clawing your way up the career ladder, pointless politics and competition, and seeing who can own more of everything? Forget about scoring and concentrate on living!

Just remember, 'He or she who dies with the most points . . . still dies.'

9

how well is your workplace?

In theory we spend one-third of our day sleeping, one-third working and one-third 'living'. Except that these days, we often spend much more than eight hours working. How many people lie on their death beds and with their last gasp utter the words, 'I wish I'd spent more time at work'?

Very few. Because loads of people don't enjoy work. And it affects their home lives. They arrive home irritable or angry or depressed or burnt out. They believe they have lots of reasons for feeling like this. Most people take no responsibility for themselves at work. They say, 'It's the boss's fault', 'It's the system'; in fact, they blame anybody or anything but themselves. And in some cases it's true. But in most cases, the individual can approach work in a different way and find much more satisfaction and fulfilment (which leads to wellness and a happier home life).

For example, always do your own job to the best of your ability – no matter how menial it may be. Do your work in such a way that you are proud of what you do – be the best sweeper/ widget-maker/secretary/accountant/assistant/manager you can be. Strive to do better and learn more.

Be a willing student. Show some enthusiasm and initiative. If someone with more experience than you offers advice, take it with gratitude rather than resentment. Make a *big* effort to get on with other people – be thoughtful, kind and, above all, do not gossip or speak about others behind their backs. Volunteer to do courses that will increase your knowledge and effectiveness – even if you have to pay for yourself sometimes, or attend outside work hours.

In other words, treat the business as your own. Or treat your small area or domain as your own business. Run it with the same enthusiasm, vigour, excitement and commitment as if it was your own. You will be amazed at how much more you enjoy those hours at work and how much more fulfilled you are with the extra recognition you receive.

For those of you I hear crying, 'What a load of bulldust, my boss wouldn't let me do that in a million years!' or, 'Why would I work my guts out for that #@*##@?' – try this strategy. If *you* take responsibility for yourself and your own fulfilment at work (a great wellness habit), you have a much better chance of enjoying the place and activities that occupy the largest part of your life.

In all cases it's true that the culture of the organisation – no matter how small – has a dramatic impact on the attitude of the people working there. And the culture of any organisation is determined largely by the Big Boss. Smaller bosses (managers down the line) create their own subculture, but this is still affected by the overall organisational culture.

The impact of the culture within a place was driven home to me when I visited Blackmore's in Sydney. It was a fantastic place to spend some time in, let alone work in! They are a company that manufactures a range of natural products, from vitamins to beauty products.

It was the enthusiasm of the whole place that captured me – everyone there is excited by what they do. They are all committed to the values of the company, which are based on offering the safest, best and most effective natural products for their customers.

Their research and development department is committed to looking for the latest, validated new findings. They fund university research projects, and conduct seminars all over the country because they are committed to furthering the knowledge of naturopaths and the general public. They have a naturopathic clinic on site and offer a free phone advisory service that takes 60 000 calls a month! Now that's what I call a company committed to helping the community. And the staff know it and love it. They feel that what they are doing really helps people; that the effort and hours they put in make a difference.

Not only that, but Blackmore's shows it values the wellness of its employees and recognises their contribution. There is a canteen offering a range of subsidised, healthy and delicious foods – not the normal stodgy or 'junk' food most workplace canteens offer. (Sorry, canteens, but it's mostly true.) And a gymnasium that is fully equipped and has a full-time coordinator/adviser. (For the cynics, 25 per cent of the staff use the gym every day and up to 60 per cent use it at varying times – so the culture fosters the use of this wellness facility.) There is a 'shop' on site offering discounted Blackmore's products to employees. But wait – there's more!

Marcus Blackmore, the Big Boss, is a delightful, approachable man who knows everyone by name. He is obviously respected and admired by his team, whom he respects. And he has a group of dedicated, excited, enthusiastic, energetic, committed, creative people in 'his family'. Do you think he is just lucky?

No. Of course not. As any Big Boss, or 'middle boss' or even 'small boss' needs to, he has worked hard to define the values of the organisation. And to make sure everyone knows those values. There is a commitment to his team, the community, education, research and honesty. His people are proud to sell the products and proud to be associated with the company. They feel appreciated (a huge wellness/productivity-related feature). This in turn creates an environment in which people 'blossom' and develop.

Any organisational, departmental or sectional leader who attempts to create an environment in which people can grow, and develop, and be the best they can be will see communication, enthusiasm, laughter and productivity soar.

And any individual who, despite having a despotic, power-crazed, uncommunicative, divide-and-conquer, unfulfilled, miserable sort of manager, takes responsibility for themselves to do the best they can and be the best they can be in any circumstances will be happier, sleep better and stay well. Sometimes, of course, it's better to find another job – then be the best you can be.

So ask yourself, 'How well is my workplace?' and, 'What culture have I created?' and, 'What can I do to make it better for me – and my team?' Then do it and reap the rewards – both personal and professional.

physical
wellness

1

does your body talk to you?

Yes! Yes! and Yes! We have never been taught to listen to it. Rarely does pain suddenly burst into your body – unless you are hit by a truck! We are always given a series of warning signs. But we are not taught what the warning signs are. So here they are . . .

The warning signs your body gives you when you are about to do damage are burning, tingling, tightness, stiffness, numbness, heaviness, dragging, pulling or discomfort. By the time you feel pain, it's usually too late. The damage is done and you have to undo it and *then* restore the normal state of the tissues.

If you are tuned into the burning, tingling, tightness, stiffness, numbness, heaviness, dragging, pulling or discomfort and become aware of any of these, the second (or minute) they occur, you can almost always do something to eliminate them. Easily.

Most of these warning signs occur because we hold our bodies in one position for too long. This generally reduces the blood flow through the muscles and tissues, particularly if the muscle is being used statically. That means that the muscle tightens and stays tight to perform the activity. It cuts off its own blood supply. And soon you will feel the warning signs. Often you will be unaware that you even experience these signs until someone brings them to your attention.

How long is too long? More than about 20 minutes is too long. Some research done at the Australian National University a couple of years ago demonstrated that muscle fatigue started after about 20 minutes of use, even though it was not obvious to the user. The whole limb didn't start shaking with fatigue after 20 minutes, but there were definite signs of fatigue within the muscle, and if you kept working or using the muscle in the same way you would soon feel the warning signs.

This means that after 20–30 minutes of performing any activity, no matter how fantastic you feel, you should stop for a second and stretch to relax the muscles. Allow them to recover by restoring their blood supply.

It's important that people realise the significance of the warning signs and the control these messages give them over their body and its aging and wellbeing. Your body talks to you all the time and gives you countless opportunities to balance it and protect it. Our society is not geared to this way of thinking – we just keep using and abusing our bodies until they 'break'! And then we complain. We often take better care of our cars than our bodies.

How many people would let their car become so dirty that the paintwork is affected? Or continue using the car, never giving it a service, until the engine seized up and had to be replaced? Or waited till a tyre was so thin it blew up rather than replacing the tyre when it was looking worn? Not many people are that ignorant of cars and safety. Yet most of us treat our bodies very differently. We expect our bodies to keep on keeping on with no attention or service or maintenance.

Unfortunately, our bodies don't work that way. They need to be taken care of on a preventative basis. They need special treatment to stay flexible, young, vital and energetic. The majority of people claim they don't have time to do the things they know they should do (like exercising, resting, playing, meditating, sitting and doing nothing); but it's really a matter of priorities and organisation. If only people understood that they would have extra time if they were fit (1.5 hours more per day usually because you need about that much less sleep when you are fit); that they would have more energy and vitality; they would feel younger; their bodies wouldn't ache or hurt any more; they could play sport again, and so on.

There is a way you can know when you have reached your body's limit and you *have* to do something to restore the balance. That way is listening to the warning signs. And when you are aware of them, stop and ask yourself, 'What do I need to do right now to restore my body or life balance?' Listen for the answer and then take a few moments to do whatever you need to do.

The following activities help restore balance:

- stretch in the opposite direction from the one in which you were just using your body
- relax your body by moving it in all directions for a couple of minutes (or perhaps hours!)
- do some more dynamic exercise
- deep breathe
- lighten up
- laugh
- go outside and feel the sunshine
- jog on the spot for a minute
- move more often – keep changing the way you are using the muscles by changing tasks or activity.

The more you tune into your body, the more amazed you'll be at how easy it is to make yourself feel active, energetic and younger.

2

a happy body

How happy are you with your physical wellness? Not just your body shape! In fact, focusing on and being obsessed and unhappy with our too fat, too thin, too tall, too short (in our opinion) body is one of the most prevalent diseases of our society.

Physical wellness goes far beyond just our body shape.

Sit quietly for a while, and then ask yourself, 'How much energy and vitality do I have? How much do I want? How is my body shape? If I am not happy with it, what would I prefer? How is my muscle tone? Are my muscles weak and flabby or firm and tight? Am I cardiovascularly (heart–lung) fit? And how fit would I like to be? Is my life too sedentary? Do I smoke? Or drink or do anything else to excess? Do I want to give up or change some habits? Do I have arthritis? Is my heart happy?'

In other words, what am I happy with and what would I like to change?

If you are really happy with your physical wellness – fantastic! If not, work out what you are willing to do about it. Let's take it chunk by chunk – the easiest way to eat an elephant is piece by piece! (By the way, if you haven't exercised for a couple of months, have a check-up with your doctor first.)

1. If you don't wake up most (OK, some) mornings full of energy and vitality, ask yourself, 'Why not?'

Possible Solutions: Do you need more sleep; less alcohol; less stress; better food; more exercise; more love; less work or just more life? We are our own best doctors in many cases – when we stop long enough to be still and quiet most of us really do have a sense of what we need. And what we need *to do* – there's a big difference! Sometimes what we need is to do nothing for a while!

Once you have identified what you need to do, set a goal and make a plan of easy and achievable steps to help you to reach that goal. Set a time frame – both a start and a finish date – or you'll never do it.

2. What about your body shape? Is the feature you would like to change genetic and unchangeable or made especially by you? Being overweight in many cases requires tremendous hard work and dedication – putting vast amounts of food (when you are not hungry) in your mouth takes determination!

    Possible solutions: Go to the gym, join a yoga group, start circuit training, attend body-building classes, eat less, eat much less. Exercise more, learn about your body and how it works, and the best nutrition for it; do not diet – no fads, watch what you put in your mouth; visualise what you want to look like every morning; think of yourself as that shape already; when eating ask yourself, 'Does my mouth want this or my stomach?'; gradually change the way and the amount and the type of food you eat. It is important to chew each mouthful at least 30 times. Not only does this prepare the foods for digestion, it prepares your stomach for the oncoming digestive process. And it makes you feel full; try it, it's not easy – at least 30 chews!

3. If your muscles are flabby and soft then you have poor muscle tone. Good muscle tone is what you see on athletes – firm, non-sagging, hard muscles. Age doesn't mean we automatically have to fall into flabby mode; it just means we stopped exercising certain muscle groups, like abdominals

and triceps muscles, to name a couple. If you want to turn your body clock back ten years and look that much younger, work on muscle tone.

Possible solutions: Lift weights, do more yoga, go to the gym for specific body-building sessions; do aerobic exercises; walk and do upper limb exercise while you walk; walk or run up and down stairs a lot; do sit-ups and push-ups at home; find a personal trainer you like.

4.   What about cardiovascular fitness? Do you puff and pant walking up slight hills or collapse after two flights of stairs? Not good, team! We need aerobic fitness to keep our body – and brain – in peak condition. Being aerobically fit means we have buckets of oxygen available for the brain (which sucks up more oxygen than any other organ) and for our muscles. Wanna live longer? Then get fit and build up your muscle strength.

Possible solutions: Work your way up to walking four kilometres in 30 minutes at least four times a week; walking burns more fat than running – good news!; go for a swim four times a week or do exercises that make you puff in the pool for 30 minutes; use a skipping rope – fabulous exercise; go for a run (if you have to); ride a bike – real or stationary; walk on a treadmill; run up and down stairs; hire a personal trainer. There are a zillion things you can do to be aerobically fit, and you know most of them: as Nike says – just do it!

Do the exercise so that you are working at a perceived rate of exertion that is enough for you. The level at which you exercise is determined by how you feel – when you feel you are going fast enough or hard enough, that's where you keep it!

5.   Is your life very sedentary? Ha, ha – only if you live in the twenty-first century! Even if you work standing up, unless you are moving rapidly all day and puffing as you go, you are not in an active job – you are in a job where you can move. Most people sit down for 30 years of their working lives – no

wonder they are tired! Sedentary lifestyles increase your risk of bowel cancer by 60 per cent – not good! If you are a complete slob, the good news is that doing some form of activity will have astounding effects on how you feel and your health. So get moving!

Possible solutions: Stand up and stretch every 30 minutes; go for a brisk walk at lunchtime; use the stairs instead of the lift; walk to the shop; don't drive; stop using the remote control and walk to the TV instead; stop watching the TV and play sport at night; run around the garden with your children; vigorously scrub the bathroom or kitchen; move more; push the mower and do the gardening instead of paying someone to do it so you can sit longer!

6.   You'll only want to give up smoking if you have a brain! Often it's difficult to give up even if you have a brain. So make a decision that you are a non-smoker and keep repeating it – you are the only one who can stop yourself. See yourself drinking tea, coffee or alcohol without the cigarette in your hand. Watch what you say to yourself about you and your smoking – you may be programming yourself to keep smoking by telling yourself you're addicted. Of course it's not that simple, but this is a good start. The same applies to other addictions like drinking or drugs.

You could try my good friend Dr John Tickell's approach of three alcohol-free days a week – preferably in a row. If that proves to be a huge struggle, then you might have a 'problem'. Or just adopt his philosophy of 'moderation man/woman' – do what you like but set a limit and stick to it.

7.   If you are riddled with or vaguely bothered by arthritis, listen up! There's lots you can do. Put simply, arthritis is when two bones rub against each other – the 'cushion' between them has gone. So inflammation and pain arise from the grinding of bone on bone. And then the pain stops you using the joints, so the muscles weaken; which puts more strain on the joints; which increases inflammation; which increases pain,

and so on. The only way to stop the spiral is to gently exercise on a daily basis and bring back joint mobility and muscle strength. Initially you may need some physiotherapy to loosen stuck joints and to be taught appropriate exercises but then it's up to you to maintain the programme.

You can make a dramatic difference to how you feel and your levels of pain. Study your diet and watch a video called *A Diet For All Reasons* from the Vegetarian Society in your state. Learn about the food you eat and its influence on the inflammation in your body and adjust your diet accordingly. Exercise in a pool until the joints and muscles are strong enough to work out of water. Make sure you have enough essential fatty acids in your diet. Not all fats are bad – read *Fats that Cure, Fats that Kill* by Udo Erasmus. Above all, keep mobile and moving.

Rheumatoid arthritis is similar but the approach needs to be much more gentle and slow.

8. Other things I haven't been able to think of – only you can know! And only you can determine what you need to do to remedy the situation.

So there are a load of ideas to start you on your path to physical wellness. You will be 'killing two birds with one stone' in many cases, like increasing cardiovascular fitness while improving muscle tone and body shape, simultaneously.

If you have many points to work on, then prioritise them. Choose one area that you would be willing to work with for a few weeks, and draw up a schedule that's workable for you. Plan it sensibly; wellness is not about expecting huge changes. It's gradual – progress may come in spurts or waves, but consistent gradual improvement is the best goal for most. Plan reviews of your progress every month and celebrate when you have reached your target.

Make the commitment to your body happpiness – no one else will!

Oh yes, remember to have fun!

3

posture and happiness

I t's time to explore another aspect of physical wellness – our posture. Posture as we stand, sit, work and study. And the warning signs our bodies give us when we are about to do damage.

Other than when our parents nagged us as teenagers, or when we admire a gorgeous body, when do we consciously think about posture? Not very often. We resented our parents' interference and to be cool we slouched even more, so we could be exactly like our spotty peers! If a person has poor, unbalanced posture, we don't turn our heads with an admiring glance because it's not gorgeous to look at!

Poor and unbalanced posture is one of the most insidious causes of pain and discomfort. Because the knee bone is connected to the thigh bone, etc. when we stand with our feet splayed like Charlie Chaplin, our pelvis thrust forward, our shoulders hunched and spine rounded and chin poked forwards (umm, doesn't this sound attractive?), we place enormous stresses on the joints and ligaments of our whole body. Not to mention that we look like gorillas!

And before long we begin to experience burning, tingling, tightness, stiffness, numbness, heaviness, dragging, discomfort and pulling – the warning signs our bodies give us to let us know that something is amiss, that damage is imminent. Unfortunately, most people are completely unaware of these signs because they are not used to listening to their bodies. So the signals become stronger and stronger until they can no longer be ignored or pain explodes.

Take a step towards wellness today and pay attention to the messages your body is giving you. Be especially alert to those warning signs I mentioned. As soon as they appear, notice what position your body is in and adjust it – if you have been in one position for more than about 20 minutes, reverse that position. If you have ever painted a ceiling, you'll know what I mean! We hold our neck at an extreme angle as we stare up to see what we are doing and the second we return it to normal position, the pain is excruciating! And all we had to do to avoid this was to look down – do the opposite movement – every 20 minutes.

Be aware of your body position and reverse any position you have been in for 20 minutes.

So back to our day-to-day posture – the way we stand and sit. This often leads to back and neck pain and, in my opinion, our thoracic spine is the key. That's the area between our shoulder blades – the bit that curves out to make a hunchback. Have you seen that big lump at the base of the neck in a lot of older people (and, unfortunately, much younger people now)? Well, that's the fourth and fifth neck bones slowly fusing, because we have a slouched thoracic spine which makes us poke out our chin, which in turn compresses those two bones. Neck discomfort and pain ensue – not to mention that it makes us look like dorks!

Here's a simple exercise that will help free up those two joints – it's especially good to do this exercise when you feel any warning signs. I call it 'the turkey'! (As usual, be checked by a health professional before you start the exercises.) Keep your chin parallel to the floor and, sitting or standing straight, pull your face in. Seriously, slide your chin gently backwards so you develop a double chin and you will feel the joints in your neck slowly stretching. The more you do this (gently) the better your neck will feel.

There is an easy exercise that will help you unbend your

thoracic spine. Sit in a chair with a backrest that stops just under your shoulder blades; stretch your arms up in the air and rock backwards over the back of the chair. Make sure the chair is stable and the stretch gentle! Do this exercise, called 'the rack', as often as you can during the day – you'll love the effects.

If you have pain doing any of these exercises, do them smaller so there is no pain. (Pain is nature's warning. It is saying 'you need to do this, but smaller'. However, if it hurts to do even very slight movements, seek medical advice before you continue.)

What about standing – how can we be balanced and look good again? Firstly, take off all your clothes except your underwear and stand side on to a full length mirror. Use a hand held mirror to see what you look like – notice the position of your feet, hips, lower back, thoracic spine, shoulders and chin. Then see what you look like from the front. If this doesn't give you the motivation to change, then your posture must be pretty good!

If you decide you would like to look elegant, taller, impressive, or just plain old good, there is an easy four-step process. The steps are simple; remembering to do it is not!

Step one: Make your feet parallel and four inches/10 centimetres apart – this frees up your pelvis.

Step two: Imagine you have a clock on the side of your pelvis with 4 o'clock at the front and 8 o'clock at the back. Most people stand with a sway back – their bums stuck out at 8 o'clock. We need to rock our pelvis from 8 o'clock to 4 o'clock and keep it there; this takes strain off the lower back.

Step three: Imagine you have a piece of elastic connecting your navel with a spot between your nipples. Without breathing in, elongate that elastic – in other words, stretch your torso but keep your shoulders relaxed. Most people take in a huge breath and tense their shoulders as they try to do this. Wrong! Concentrate on keeping relaxed. And keep breathing normally.

Step four: Clasp your hands lightly behind your bottom. Keeping your shoulders relaxed, gently stretch your hands towards the floor. This will help to open up your chest.

By now you may be feeling like someone has strapped a broomstick to your back! And you may feel horribly uncomfortable – but the mirror will show you that you look terrific! And if you feel for that lump at the base of the neck it will be gone or much smaller. Persevere, because you will soon find this position more comfortable than your usual slump – you'll have less discomfort and more energy and you may even notice people watching you with admiration! As an added extra, you'll feel happier – mood and posture are closely linked.

4

exercise and you

I doubt that there would be one person in the Western world today who doesn't know that exercise is important for the body, mind and soul. Unless they live in a bubble and have not listened to radio or TV or read a newspaper in the last forty years.

But I don't think they understand just *how* important it is. Or more people would do it. It's not just your heart and lungs that benefit from exercise, it's every organ in your body: your liver, kidney, spleen, bowels, bladder and skin, to name a few. It's fantastic for busting stress and boosting energy. It's good for your soul and recharges your spirit.

If you were given a magnificent car – a Ferrari or 800 series BMW or whatever you think is a wonderful machine – would you lock it up in the garage and never use it? If you did, you would soon notice that this wonderful machine had been ruined by the inactivity. Engines need to be run; they need oil pumping through all the moving bits.

The human body is the most impressive machine of all – it needs oil of different types pumping through the joints, muscles, cells, brain, kidneys, heart and other parts. And the old adage of 'use it or lose it' is true. Inactivity is the enemy of the human machinery. Sedentary lifestyles contribute to more disease than you can imagine – not just boring old heart disease, but cancer, arthritis, chronic fatigue and most diseases you can think of.

Have you ever had this experience? You arrive home after work exhausted. You have been sitting all day but you are still exhausted. All you want to do is to flop into another chair, drink heavily and watch TV. Suddenly, you remember you promised to go out and exercise with someone that night. You make 84 phone calls trying to get out of the arrangement. You can't. So you drag yourself out, cursing your stupidity.

What are you like when you return? Aren't you bursting with energy, vim and vigour? You spring back home feeling ready to clean the house, write eight reports or party for three days! There's a message here! You leave home feeling spent and drained; you exercise and arrive home feeling wonderful.

Did you know that when you are fit, or at least active, and you smoke, the bad effects of the smoking are reduced? In fact, the damage done by any bad health habit is lessened if you exercise. The incidence of cancer is lower in people who exercise regularly. Stress levels are lower and life flows more easily. They keep their perspective on life and events happening to them. Fit people have better relationships and higher self-esteem; they laugh more and yes – they even have more orgasms! (From a recent review of women who exercise regularly.)

Have I given you enough information yet to make you rush out the door and start exercising? If not, keep reading! In the past we thought humans had to exercise heavily several times a week to be fit and that being very fit was the best possible state. Too much exercise can lead to all sorts of hormonal disturbances, free radical and physical damage, and can be addictive. But too little exercise is just as bad.

The Cooper Aerobic Clinic is the largest and best-known exercise research centre in the world and they tell us that, for moderate to reasonable fitness, all we need to do is walk four kilometres in 30 minutes, four times a week. Yes, it is possible – I do it most mornings! And no, I haven't made a mistake. If the area you walk in is very hilly then you could walk less in

30 minutes for the same impact. If you want to be very fit they suggest walking four kilometres in 20 minutes four times a week.

Now, that's not too hard. You don't need expensive gear, training, gym subscriptions, a personal trainer or to perform in front of anyone. All you need is walking shoes and a place! If you don't have a place, use a treadmill. Instead of watching the news go for a four-kilometre walk. Take your family – model a wellness behaviour for your children. The best way to instil health habits in your children is to have the children see you exercising, eating well and indulging in other healthy habits.

Of course, you can do any sort of exercise you like. Maybe you prefer bike riding or swimming (it's great to meditate as you swim), or gym work or circuit training or jogging on a trampoline, or some running or tennis or golf (but you have to walk fast on the green!) or any physical activity you can think of.

But wait, there's more! Even better news. The absolute slob – the person who hasn't used a muscle in 30 years; who can't remember when they last exercised – is the person who benefits the most! And all they have to do is *some* physical activity – for 10 minutes, three times a day. That's all! According to recent research from the Pennsylvania State University (The Noll Physiological Research Centre) every adult should accumulate 30 minutes or more of moderately intensive physical activity per day. It can be in one hit or it can be accumulated in short bouts.

This means take the stairs instead of the lift; garden for a while; walk short distances instead of driving; scrub the bathroom tiles vigorously; take the washing up and down the stairs in small bundles more frequently; walk to the TV instead of using the remote control! Think of all the ways you could combine vigorous activity with your daily life.

Apparently, the health benefits for the slob who starts being active are astounding! If you are already fit, you will still benefit from the exta exercise, but the results will be less dramatic.

If I haven't convinced you to start doing some exercise, you're still in the bubble! Good luck.

5

how to motivate yourself to exercise

Are you someone who is motivated by determining a goal you want to achieve and moving towards it? Or someone who decides what they don't want and then 'moves away' from that? In other words does the threat of a negative consequence drive you into action or do you promise yourself a reward when you have completed something?

Do you get out of bed because you have to, or because you are excited about what the day has to offer?

This may take a little bit of soul searching, but it's worth the effort. Think back to times in your life when you have been really committed to doing something. What motivated you at that time? What did you tell yourself about what you wanted to do? Did you see yourself having achieved the goal? Or were you driven by *not* wanting to be somewhere or something else? Or maybe you felt it would be great to leave the old situation behind?

Take a few minutes and make some notes about those situations, especially the point at which you remember making the decision to do something or making the commitment, whatever it was. Perhaps it was to give up smoking, to lose weight, learn a new skill or change some aspect of your life. Make sure you choose something at which you were successful; otherwise your motivation strategy (as it's called) will not be the best one to repeat!

Now, think about regular exercise. What do you see, say to

yourself or feel? Very few people sit back and think, 'Yes, great! Regular exercise, what fun!' But most people know regular exercise is the best way to achieve the health goals they have.

How *do* you get yourself excited about exercise? Or even to the point where you will do it?

One way is to think about the previous paragraphs, then sit down and write out and draw pictures (stick figures or symbols) of what you want to achieve. Be very specific. Describe how you would look, sound and feel once you have achieved your outcome – *as if* you had already achieved it.

Then think about and write and draw what you don't want to be – or what you are now. Describe this very specifically – how you would look, sound and feel if you continued with your current behaviours.

(It is important to remember that we're talking about behaviours here. We're not talking about changing your whole personality, just some behaviours.)

And then think about what has to happen to move you from what you don't want or what you are now to what you want to be.

Let me give you an example. Let's say you want to lose weight. How much weight would you like to lose? What reasons do you have for wanting to lose that weight? (I want to look better, have more energy, lower my cholesterol, improve my arthritis, fit into my clothes, look more sexy, etc.) Now list your reasons for staying at the same weight. (I'm safe, it cost me a lot to put on this weight, I won't need a new wardrobe, I'm cuddly, I'm happy, it's too hard to lose weight, etc.)

If you have been 'trying' to lose weight forever and don't seem to keep it off even when you do lose it, see if you can work out if there is a part of you that really wants to keep the weight on – and for what reason. Be honest with yourself!

Then describe what you would look, sound and feel like if it had already happened. Use positive phrases like: I look slim (not 'I would not have a beer gut'!), I am smiling and hearing comments from others about how good I look; I bounce through the day with loads of energy and really look forward to my exercise – or enjoy doing it once I start; I feel good and confident about myself. Be as descriptive and detailed as you like.

OK, now the move away. Right now, I look flabby. I feel sluggish and embarrassed. My confidence is gone – people whisper things about how big I am. My clothes are tight and make me feel uncomfortable. I am not very sexy. This part is sometimes easier than the positive stuff!

Next list the reasons (excuses) you give yourself for not exercising – not enough time, too hard, I sweat and get dirty, etc. – and ask yourself if these are really valid reasons. Be honest!

Then list what benefits you will gain from regular exercise. By now you are ideally ready to tackle this new goal of making regular exercise and habit and possibly even fun!

Start with small chunks as you plan the goal you are after.

1. Think about how you could find four lots of 30 minutes in the next week. Maybe you could avoid the evening news and do it then. Perhaps you could wake up 30 minutes earlier (it gets easier after a couple of weeks) or take the dog for a walk or, better still, the children. This way they see their parents behaving in a 'wellness' way and then they model or copy what you do. This is the way children take in about 70 per cent of everything they learn – watching (not listening to) you! Perhaps it could become a family activity. Your partner or a friend could support you in reaching your goal.

2. Choose some activity that you can do and might even enjoy. Walk, cycle, go to the gym, swim, skip, etc. Or are you a team person? Do you prefer to exercise with others or to be competitive?

3. Think about the rewards you will give yourself at the end of the week when you have done four lots of exercise. (Not chocolates!)

4. Create some way of monitoring your progress to give

yourself feedback. Be aware that as you exercise you build up muscle and muscle is heavier than fat. So the scales may show that you have put on weight but you notice your clothes fit better or that your shape has changed. Look for these changes rather than just weight loss.

5.   Then plan the next week. Think of ways you could make the exercise fun – listen to a walkman, play your favourite music or tapes that will teach you new skills, play with the children or the dog while you exercise, meditate as you exercise, etc.

6.   If you are not enjoying the exercise, try to work out the reasons. And maybe change the way you do it or find another form of exercise. Keep in mind it often takes two or three weeks before you develop some fitness, at which point the exercise becomes a little easier.

7.   Frequently assess where your motivation is. Think of a scale from 1–10 where 1 is 'I never want to exercise again' and 10 is 'I'm hooked'. Keep track of where you are and if you start sliding down the scale work out the reasons and be creative about how you can build up your levels again. Once you see and feel a little success your motivation improves dramatically!

Spend some time thinking about how you think about motivation! Discuss it at dinner parties! Ask your children – create an awareness in them that they have control over how motivated they are. Have some fun with the thinking process!

6

mindbody medicine

If you think we have a body that houses a mind (amongst other things) and that the two are separate, think again! For many years scientific research has shown conclusively, in many different ways, that the mind and the body are in fact the 'same'. We have a bodymind – we can think with all our organs! It's just that we may not be able to understand the language of our stomach or our heart. They often 'talk' to us and because we are not tuned into their 'dialect' or signs, we miss their important messages.

There are even scientifically recognised fields of study in this arena, called mindbody medicine, psychoneuroimmunology and cardiopsychoneuro-immunology (cardio-psycho-neuro-immunology, meaning the study of the interrelationship of the mindbody and the heart and immune system).

Did you know that the immune system of the bodymind is its army against disease? AIDS doesn't kill people. AIDS kills the immune system, which then allows any old germ to whip into our bodies and destroy us. While we have a healthy and optimally functioning immune system, we are in the best state to fight colds, flus or any other diseases. Boosting our immune systems is a much underrated pastime!

Traditionally, we focus on various health aspects for various specific reasons. Like diet now or be fat forever and have a heart attack. Or stop smoking now or your lungs will fall out! Or exercise just to 'get fit'. And they are really important steps to take. But when did you last consciously do something to boost your immune system? When did you specifically rush out and do a course on ways to boost your immune system?

You haven't, of course, because most people hadn't even heard of the immune system until AIDS became a threat. And although there is more awareness of it generally, not much is done to help people understand why it's important to have a strong immune system and how to have one.

Did you know that at any one time we have as many as 300 potential cancer cells running around our bodies? Guess what keeps them at bay? Correct – the good old immune system. Any time we become run down, stressed out, tired or just burnt out we compromise our immune systems and our battle lines against the invaders are significantly depleted.

So what attacks or weakens our immune systems? Stress is the number one enemy. The chemicals we release when we are stressed attack, in particular, the immune system. Short bursts of stress are OK – like sprinters, we can cope with short intense bursts that are infrequent. Note the word 'infrequent'! Five minutes of stress leaves your immune system weakened for six hours! Daily crises that whip your stress levels up to frenzy status for an hour or so will harm you as much as, if not more than, the very common prolonged, low-grade, ongoing sources of stress such as financial problems, family issues and unhappiness at work.

Chemotherapy is another major immune system destroyer. That's why people on chemotherapy have to be so careful to avoid others with colds or illnesses. They are far more likely to catch whatever it is than someone with a robust immune system.

Exhaustion, burn out, worry, lack of sleep and fear also give the poor old immune system a nudge. Hey, face it, just about everything we do that doesn't make us feel great will probably affect our immune systems badly!

Well then, what can we do to boost this vital system that can look after us so effectively? These strategies are easy, often cheap, take little time and leave you feeling good. Too often people in our society expect solutions to problems to be expensive, complicated and difficult. When it comes to our own wellness, that's often not the case.

For example, touch boosts the immune system. Go round hugging each other at home and you'll be boosting your own and others' immune systems! Sit close while you watch the TV. Hold hands more often. Walk arm in arm. Have a weekly massage – any sort. If you can't afford once a week then once a fortnight minimum. If that's too expensive, go with your partner or a friend and learn how to do it to each other! Then do that once a week. This is not pampering or a luxury only to be done once a year on your birthday. This is essential, critical, vital for optimum wellness. It helps you fight off disease. Children know this. How long does a toddler let you be in the house before they touch you? Minutes if you are lucky!

Social support is a fantastic boost for our immune systems – having friends and family around you, talking to your friends about problems and issues troubling you. Women are great at this. Men, you need to learn to be! It really will help you in many ways. Make sure you keep contact with your friends after you form a relationship with a significant other – we often give up our friends in favour of the 'loved one'. Big mistake. We need to blend the two and keep a balance. Have girls' nights and boys' nights. They're not such a bad idea as long as neither degenerates into a drunken orgy – I'm not sure about the negative impact of orgies on the immune system but I know that the 'drunken' is bad!

Men and women rarely find a friend or mate of the opposite sex with whom they can openly discuss everything in a non-emotional environment. So in my opinion, cultivating same-sex friendships that allow, indeed encourage, you to talk about feelings, worries and concerns are great for the immune system.

And now, for another simple, remarkably effective immune system booster: laughter. Yes, common old garden-variety mirth, chuckling and particularly belly-aching laughter! Not only do you feel great after a gut-busting laugh that brings tears to your eyes – you are also healthier.

Watching a comedy video has been shown to boost the immune system. But watching a 'boysy' type movie – one that has large numbers of guns, loads of blood and violence, speed and suspense – lowers the strength of your immune system – for up to five hours after the movie! So unless you think that sort of movie is a comedy then either don't watch them or don't go anywhere near anyone who is sick for five hours afterwards! And the next time you think you might be heading for the flu, rent out five comedies and laugh yourself to wellness!

Anything you can do that reduces stress boosts your immune system. Exercise, meditation, having a bath, walking in the bush, sitting quietly, deep breathing, listening to relaxing music, looking at water, sailing, playing golf, reading – whatever you can do that helps you relax will boost your immune system.

Help someone. Studies have shown that when we help others we actually boost our immune systems. So do the washing up; remember to pick up the dry-cleaning; mow the lawn for an older next-door neighbour; do something you have not been asked to do that will help someone at work or at home; ask people what you can do to help them and then do it! You're helping two people – yourself and the other!

See – I said the ways to build your immune system could be quick, cheap, effective! And these are only some of the many ways you can do it. Make a commitment to yourself to do something every day that you know will boost your disease-fighting system. You'll be amazed at how you are suddenly the only one who 'never catches colds'!

7

men and health

Why do men die so much earlier than women? We women are not physiologically superior – just mentally (just kidding, guys; keep your sense of humour – it helps you live longer!).

Fellas, you don't have to die so early! After all, most medical research has been done on men. Medicine used to be a male-dominated profession and there are enormous amounts of information available on lifestyle and health and its effect on men . . . so what's the matter with you?

Why do most of you make your poor mothers, partners, lovers, female friends and children nag you about unsafe habits? Why don't you stop smoking? exercise more? eat better? And relax. Laugh more. Be silly and have fun. Why are you so wimpy when you have a minor illness, and when you're really sick we don't know until you're dead? Why do you take notice when a complete stranger tells you what to do, but you accuse us of nagging?

Wellness is when we wake up with energy and vitality; women are good at ensuring everyone else's wellness, but they're not especially efficient at looking after their own. But we are more aware of ourselves than men. Traditional approaches to health involve waiting until something goes wrong, then doing something about it. Men are spectacular at this!

Women (generally speaking, of course!) are into wellness. Women tend to notice earlier than men that something is wrong with them. Before something actually falls off.

Unfortunately, women have a 'martyr gene'! Which means that when we have stopped worrying about everyone else, what they are doing, eating and feeling, we have time for ourselves and we may seek help. We have noticed something is wrong, it's just that we don't allocate time to seek help earlier.

Men, on the other hand, work well on the basis of crises. Men are often oblivious to the fact that anything is wrong. Until it's too late! A man will wait until he's in intensive care or doubled up in agony or can't walk any more before he seeks help. Or complies with the advice he has sought or been given.

I wonder if men really think about the consequences of their actions at the time. Do you guys realise that when you are really enjoying a cigarette or the buzz from overwork, you are creating internal havoc? I think many men choose to ignore what they know to be true. Like affairs. Some men will choose immediate gratification over thinking about the likely outcome of their behaviour.

If someone says to a woman, 'You need to drink more water to flush out your kidneys', she usually complies. Tell a man the same thing and you tell him every hour for three days before you give up in frustration, as he tells you not to nag him!

Women are generally more likely to take up regular wellness-promoting activities like yoga, meditation, walking, seeing friends, talking about problems, etc. We'll read books on improving diet, state of mind, health and relationships and if we're lucky, when we suggest he read the same books, he'll say 'just read me the relevant bits'! If we're really lucky, he'll listen!

Yoga, most men think, is a wimp activity. Wrong! My Iyengar yoga teacher is as strong as any man I know and has a great body – all from yoga. He's 52 and has the face and body of a 40-year-old. So for those men out there brave enough to have read this far, if you have any aches or pains or want to improve the shape of your body and feel great and younger at the same time, take up Iyengar yoga. It's fabulous exercise and keeps you flexible and fit. And often eliminates back pain.

Or take up walking four kilometres in 30 minutes. Yes, it is possible and you can do it! It keeps you fit, strengthens your muscles and helps you relax. Do it instead of watching the TV at night.

Having presented at several conferences held by The Young Presidents Organisation, a worldwide organisation of young, very successful people (mostly men), I know that some men who are exposed to vast amounts of information focusing on their health and its connection to their performance do actually make changes! Of course, being exposed to this information repeatedly does help.

Lots of these men meditate. Yes, it's true. Of course, if it was public knowledge that meditation helps relaxation and productivity, lessens the risk of heart attack, lowers blood pressure, reduces the long-term impact of stress, improves concentration, creativity and imagination, increases energy and output, improves sleep and allows you to communicate better, maybe we would have more men allocating 20 minutes a day to this incredibly beneficial activity. It probably also improves your sex life. (That should increase the number of men willing to meditate regularly!) Golf is better than a poke in the eye with a sharp stick, but it doesn't do for you what yoga and meditation can. (And anyway, meditation will probably improve your golf game!)

Recently, a doctor friend of mine told me the most effective way to stop men smoking was to inform them that smoking increases the risk of impotence (true). In a big (so to speak) way. Every cigarette we smoke instantly reduces the size of all our blood vessels. This means less blood pumps around the body. When certain parts of the body need hydraulic pressure (as it does) and the blood vessels can't carry enough blood, you know what happens! Or, speaking more accurately, what doesn't happen.

Men need to learn to talk about their feelings – after they become aware of what they are feeling. No joke, many of us have lost contact with our feelings in the search for money and the race to live with more possessions. Try keeping a diary. Both women who are working and raising a family and busy career women are losing our natural female ability to tap into our own feelings. Being aware of and sharing feelings has a dramatic impact on heart disease. It reduces the chance of heart attack. I can imagine some cynics reading this and muttering, 'If we started to talk about feelings it would open a can of worms!' Good. As long as we deal with them wisely. See a psychologist if you're struggling to cope on your own. It's smart, not a stigma.

Testosterone seems to bring inbuilt competition and risk taking, both of which seem to add to the list of health hazards associated with being male. Perhaps it could be put to good purpose – fellas, take a risk and be different from the rest! Be responsible for your diet and health *before* you find yourself in the situation where there is permanent damage.

Remember to take your vitamins, if you need them, without expecting someone else to put them in front of you. Eat muesli or porridge. Eating any sort of breakfast is critical to wellness. Make enquiries for yoga by yourself and go to classes without having to be prompted. Explore meditation and practice it daily. Read the books – and not just the relevant bits!

Of course, there will be zillions of men who are already doing this – good on you, fellas! You are extending your life – and that of your partner. She will live a lot longer and be much happier without the responsibility and strain of constant nagging (she nags because she doesn't want you to die early!) and without having to watch your face distort with repulsion as you swallow something healthy!

Anyway, all the above will improve your sex life. I promise!

8

the bum

Well, I bet most of you have been waiting for this. An opportunity to find out about the intricacies of your innermost ... bowels. Yes, your inner derrière.

Bowel cancer is all too common in our society. It's a real problem that affects most households in some way, at some stage in their lives. Especially if there is a family history. So why are we not spreading the word on 'bum wellness'? Why do we only give people the 'warning signs of bowel cancer' – the signs that tell you there is already something wrong in a major way?

How many people wake up in the morning and utter these immortal words, 'I wonder how my bum is this morning?' Not many. But we should! Most people never spend 30 seconds thinking about the wellness of their bottom bits until one day they go to the toilet and suddenly ... 'oooh, that didn't feel right'; they have a look and, terrified, off they rush to the doctor who says, 'Sorry, it's too late'.

Anyway, enough about the down side – let's look at how we can keep our bum in great shape and know that it is. After many discussions with specialists, I have discovered this well-kept secret: you will know your bum is in great shape when you have ... (drum roll) ... fluffy floaties. There, I said it. Out loud and in public. Fluffy floaties are essential – as opposed to stinky sinkies. If you are one of those people who comes out of the loo and calls out, 'Don't go in there for a week!' you are in fact, in deep doo doo. And you *must* eat more fibre, fruit, vegetables,

231

bran and psyllium husks, and do some more exercise. Change your eating habits until you have those fabulous FFs.

Now, it's not just any old FFs; people after conferences rush up to me proudly proclaiming that they have to 'flush eight times'! Not good, team, because it usually means there's too much fat in there. They need to be (*warning*: I'm going to be very direct, so those of you who are squeamish out there, skip the next few lines) a standard size, a standard colour and instead of floating right on top and almost waving goodbye as you flush, or sinking solidly and rapidly straight to the bottom, they need to be 'submarines' – half way between top and bottom.

Of course, there is a little (not much) controversy about FFs and SSs. But all the doctors I spoke to liked the idea that we looked daily at what was happening 'down there' and, should we notice any change from normal, we should seek expert advice immediately. This expert advice should not come from our mates at the pub or the local ladies' reading group.

One of the reasons I proclaim the virtues of fluffy floaties as widely as I do is because it's true according to the medical experts I spoke to and it's a way of you remembering me (and this book) every day for the rest of your lives! Once someone tells you about FFs it's impossible to go to the loo again and not have just the tiniest, quickest glance to see what's happening down there!

The other aspect I'd like to bring up at this point is a difference between men and women in the nether regions. Why is it that men feel flatulence is a 'thing to be shared'? Why can't they just quietly (as women do) get on with it? And preferably escape to a distant place upwind to avoid annihilation of their partner. Why must they shake the doona to make sure that she suffocates?

Or let everyone know that they just 'can't help themselves – it had to come out.' Is it testosterone? (You are now, dear reader, wondering what sort of men I know. A good point. And of course, I'm generalising. Probably the bulk of the men out there are surrounded with women who compete with men in this flatulence arena.) Or maybe I have discovered some previously unrecognised, or long forgotten, territorial-marking, secret weapon of men. Anyway, whatever the reason I wish they would do it outside!

Oh, just one more tip. Apparently, lots of older women in particular have trouble fully emptying their bladders. The addition of a footstool that wraps around the pedestal and allows the more mature women to rest their feet and have their knees higher than their hips has a dramatic effect on the emptying of the bladder.

It also appears to help bowel movements. With our Western society sophistication, we now can sit on a throne rather than squatting over a hole in the ground (the preferred method in lower socioeconomic status countries). Most people would applaud this apparent 'advance'. But hold your acclaim. The sophisticated sitting up technique seems to 'kink' our bowel bits. So we strain and puff and exert huge pressures on that region. Not good. It hurts, it gives us haemorrhoids and we might explode. Find that footstool – you'll notice the difference!

Next time you're in the 'stress management centre for men' (toilet), instead of reading all those magazines, pile them up under your feet so your knees are higher than your hips and see how much easier the whole process becomes!

9

melanoma

It's not just 'mad dogs and Englishmen' that go out in the midday sun! It's also Aussies who are mad. As a newspaper columnist, I receive media releases on a regular basis and one arrived recently that amazed, not to mention frightened, me.

Did you know that skin cancer claims 1200 lives a year and that skin cancer accounts for 75 per cent of all cancers diagnosed annually in Australia? These figures are from the Skin and Cancer Foundation of Australia. We have the highest incidence of skin cancer in the world. And we don't know what damage we have done until it's fifteen years too late.

Unfortunately, the skin doesn't come with a radiation warning buzzer that says 'danger, danger, damage occurring', but that's what's happening. Think of lying in the sun as lying next to Chernobyl. The closer you lie to it and the longer you lie there, the more certain it is that you will be harmed. Would anyone knowingly do that? Of course not, but in many ways that's what we, our babies and teenagers are doing.

I bet most people over 30 know someone who has had skin cancers removed or who has died from melanoma. (By the way malignant melanoma is one of the most vicious cancers you can get – it's fast, and deadly.) But we are so blasé about it. Having skin cancers burned off should be treated as a warning sign that you have done plenty of damage and need to stop *now*.

Now, I know we all understand this at some intellectual level but it doesn't seem to have hit many of us at a behavioural level.

234

In other words there are still millions of idiots lying flat out like lizards in the hottest parts of the day with most of their bodies exposed to one of the most virulent carcinogens known to us!

As research for this article, I visited a beach (someone has to do it) and spent several gruelling hours observing! Not only were people baking themselves but they had babies out there baking. There were two types of umbrellas on the beach – the small ones and one 'igloo'. Everyone else had oiled themselves up so they could crisp up and look 'healthy' for summer fashion.

Very smart. Never mind that our faces look like wrinkled old prunes and the rest of our skin looks like a 50-year-old's when we are 30. Small details. This foundation had a great suggestion – look under your armpits – a sun-free zone. How wrinkled, lined or freckled are they compared with the rest of your body? Why do people from cold climates who don't see the sun much look twenty years younger than their counterparts here? And we could too. 10-year-olds in Australia are now showing signs of wrinkle sun damage around their eyes.

Guess what? If you burn six or more times during youth, you have double the chance of developing malignant melanoma. Now when I was a child and adolescent they had invented sunscreen, but the best available was zinc cream or UV cream, neither of which seems as sophisticated as the plethora of creams, potions and lotions available today. But zinc was probably effective on the grounds that nothing gets past it, not even efforts to take it off!

Forget the 'healthy tan' stuff. The only healthy tan is when we use 'fake' tanning lotion and even then, we're still adding chemicals to our poor, polluted bodies.

Now for the really disturbing news: sunscreens are not enough. They're a good start but they are not enough. The skin still burns. And the skin *does not heal*. The radiation damage festers and pops out looking like an innocent freckle or mole that we ignore until it's too late. *Then* we take notice and stay out of the sun when it's too late.

But wait, there's more. We can develop melanoma in the eye!

This usually results in removal of the whole eye. But of course, before we develop melanoma we can have cataracts, pterygiums or cancers close to the eye – all as a result of overexposure to the sun's harmful rays.

Do not ever leave the house again without your *wraparound* shades. And make sure they are good shades that cut out all the ultraviolet rays. Do not buy cheap sunglasses. Warning: children's eyes are no different from adults'. All children should be wearing them and if their parents wear sunnies, the kids are far more likely to follow suit without grumbling. This means babies' eyes too.

Just when you thought it was safe . . . baseball caps are no good as sun protection. Especially when they are worn backwards. We all need full nine-centimetre brim hats, or caps with those Lawrence of Arabia flaps at the back. Akubra type hats that block all rays are the best. Forget the old straw or thin cloth fashion type that lets plenty of those skinny little rays penetrate.

Make sure sunshades that should go over pools and play areas actually cut out the ultraviolet killers – don't use some wimpy thing that lets plenty of light through as well as the harmful rays. Remember that there is shade, and shade. Some shade cuts out the sunlight but allows the harmful rays in just fine. So make sure you are in *real* shade.

Don't relax yet . . . clothes don't necessarily protect us! Research from the Skin and Cancer Foundation shows that some light weave T-shirts have a protection factor as low as 4. This becomes even less when they become wet and stretched.

So now we have SPF – sun protection factor for creams (always go for at least 15+) and UVF – ultraviolet protection factor for clothing. Go for factor 30. When buying children's bathing suits, those full-length costumes are by far the best, but make sure you buy the genuine blockout articles, not the cheap, thin lookalikes. And stop wearing super skimpy bikinis – they really increase your chances of death. One pieces are the go; let your breasts and bottom be white – rather than not there at all!

Stop jogging without hats or shirts – but only if you have a brain and a desire to live! Stay out of the sun during the hottest part of the day. Think about children's play breaks at school. They need shade areas to play in. Who rushes out at lunchtime and covers schoolkids in factor 15?

And for goodness' sake, have an annual skin check if you are over 20 or have freckles and moles or have skin. Watch your own skin – we do breast checks (or we should), testicular checks (or we should) on a regular (monthly) basis, so why not a skin check? Notice changes, bleeding, asymmetry, border irregularity and colour variation, and if you have a mole more than six mm in diameter, watch it carefully. Apparently, 60 per cent of all melanomas are detected by the person or a relative, so start now and save yourself.

There is an epidemic of malignant melanoma. If you don't catch it early enough, the treatment really hurts. But prevention is simple. And remember, just because it's a shady day doesn't mean you are safe – exactly the same rules apply.

Remember, slip, slop, slap!

10

yoga – a secret weapon against pain

Who wants to have a body that's trim, flexible, strong and pain free and does what you want it to do, when you want it to do it? Almost everyone, of course. But why is it that so many people in our society suffer pain or discomfort and have their joints seize up, and grow old before their time? And why is back pain the worst problem?

Because we don't use our joints properly and we don't move them enough, so our brains lose the fine-tuned control over them and our muscles weaken, stretch or become tight. The whole biomechanics (how things move) of our body systems is out of kilter. Which then leaves us open and ready for injury.

What can we do about it? Yoga. That's what we can do! Before you think, 'Oh no, this time she's gone too far,' and stop reading, listen to why I'm suggesting we put it into schools and everyday life, especially for our more mature citizens.

I've been practising yoga for ten years. My yoga teacher is a bloke with a great body – better than the pumped-up body-builder sort. Peter is incredibly strong and flexible. You should see what he can make his body do! He's no wimp and doesn't dress in orange robes and eat fruit and nuts. The type of yoga we do is Iyengar yoga – it's a version that's more strenuous and physical than other forms I've tried. That's why I like it. I feel fantastic – full of energy after a class. Five or six of us go through a one and a half hour session once a week – good stretching, strengthening and balancing, and reconnecting our brains to our bodies, with a 10-minute relaxation at the end of the session.

I've been 'preaching' yoga for years now and I would like to dispel some of the many misconceptions that exist about this underrated form of exercise.

1. Yoga is not some weirdo, Indian, way-out hippie sort of thing. It's a form of exercise that gently (or as strongly as you want) stretches and strengthens your body. It has nothing to do with religion. And you wear ordinary old shorts, T-shirts, tracksuits or leotards.

2. You don't have to be female to do yoga! It's just that some men think it's a wimpy sort of thing to do, when in fact it's one of the most strenuous and beneficial forms of exercise I know. (Keep in mind, it's as strenuous as you want it to be – always work within your limits.) The other reason men do other sports is that when they attend a yoga class they are so horrified at how stiff their body is, they give up! Don't give up, guys – stick with it. You'll loosen up and will be amazed at how much better you feel and how much your tennis/golf/swimming/cricket/football (yes, even football) performance improves.

3. It takes one and a half hours every day. Wrong! I choose to go to a one and a half hour class once a week and practise selected exercises each day (or every couple of days). Ideally, I'd do a 20-minute yoga session each day.

4. It's strenuous and I need to be fit. No, you don't! You can slot into beginners, intermediate or advanced classes and work at your own rate within them. You just do what you can.

5. I have to stand on one leg or my head or balance in strange positions. Wrong again! True, some of the postures (as they name positions) you practise involve headstands and balancing on one leg (not at the same time!) but only when you're ready for it. And not at all if you don't want to.

6. All yoga teachers are the same and teach the same stuff. No, they're not! Try a few different teachers and find one that

suits you. And try a couple of different types of yoga for the one that's best for you. (There's an Iyengar Yoga Association that may be able to provide you with the names of teachers in your area.)

So if you're plagued by back pain, neck pain, arthritic aches, stiffness, or even if you feel good and want to feel better, tone up your body, free up your joints and have more energy, give yoga a try. You'll need to persist for a couple of months to give your body time to gently stretch and strengthen and then you'll feel like you have a new lease on life!

Maybe you could arrange yoga classes at lunchtime in the workplace. Or have a personal yoga trainer. Or get together a few friends on a weekly basis and have the yoga instructor come to you. Or go to a yoga centre. There are lots of options. You can even improve your cardiovascular (heart and lung) fitness levels with the stronger and more physical yoga routines. And you learn how to relax at the end of the session. You become aware of muscles you didn't even know you had. Your coordination improves. Your sports performance is enhanced. Your stress levels reduce.

Have I convinced you to 'give it a go' yet? Try it – I reckon my body is about as flexible and strong as a 23-year-old because of yoga, my sense of humour, walking and meditation. This would be not so good if I was 19, OK if I was 23 and impressive if I was 48. I think yoga's great!

11

recharge your life battery

Occasionally, we come across life-changing pieces of information. This article is about the research of Dr Johanna Budwig, a German professor, scientist and biochemist and a Nobel Prize nominee (seven times).

A research pioneer in the field of fats and cancer and health, Dr Budwig has been helping people recover from cancer without surgery or drugs since the 1950s. She has a very stringent treatment regime, her protein-rich nutrition component is well recognised in Europe and the USA, and her research has been validated by several Nobel Prize-winning scientists since.

Not only are her research findings important for cancer sufferers, they also have enormous impact on everyday wellness and peak body functioning. They can improve fertility, reduce arthritic symptoms, help diabetes, decrease some allergic reactions, minimise PMT, relieve asthma, increase feelings of relaxation and may well be the fountain of youth!

I first heard of Dr Budwig's work from an American friend who, after a career as a very successful businessman, has devoted his time to exploring the most effective ways for maximising wellness and developing our full physiological potential – in other words, how to live longer, better and happier, and neutralise the myriad of toxins that we are exposed to daily in modern lifestyles. If you are interested in this or in possibly controlling cancer or reducing your chances of developing cancer, read on!

First we need to understand the truth about fats. I'll try to simplify this as much as I can. There are 'good fats' and 'bad fats'!

The most important fact about fats is that we need them. Not all fats are bad. There are two types of fat: saturated and unsaturated. The saturated fats are found in meat, butter, eggs, fish, and chicken and are high in cholesterol. (Not so great!)

The unsaturated fats are found in either vegetable products or oils such as sunflower, sesame, safflower, corn and flaxseed (or flax) oil. They have no cholesterol and some are high in two essential fatty acids: omega 3 and omega 6 fatty acids. What we don't know and desperately need to know is that these essential fatty acids are critical for wellness – each cell in our body relies on these to reproduce without mutating and to breathe normally. We can make our own omega 6 from the foods we eat but we cannot manufacture omega 3 fatty acids (unless pregnant).

Deficiencies in omega 3 fatty acids are linked to almost all the degenerative diseases afflicting us today, as well as cancer, multiple sclerosis, chronic fatigue, diabetes, skin conditions, stress and arthritis.

The non-essential mono-unsaturated fatty acids are found in olive and other oils. These are OK – not really good or bad.

So what does this mean, you ask? It means that in our society most people need to add more highly unsaturated fats, specifically omega 3 fatty acids, to their diets.

And the best way to do this, according to Dr Budwig, Udo Erasmus (a world authority on fats and oils and author of several definitive textbooks) and several other Nobel Prize-winning scientists, is to follow this formula: once a day take one tablespoon of flaxseed oil per 45 kg of body weight. It is best if it is pure, organic and unrefined, and the sort that you must keep refrigerated and in the dark. (Australia produces some of the best flax oil in the world at Stoney Creek Oil Products.) Mix it well with one or two tablespoons of cottage cheese, yoghurt, quark or tofu (all protein) so that it emulsifies (blends completely) and eat it on your museli, toast, cereal or just by itself.

You can also add two tablespoons of flax meal if you like (except if you have coeliac disease). Some recent research suggests that flaxseed oil may be detrimental for anyone with prostate cancer, but not flax meal. This research is yet to be validated. However, you need to be extra cautious if you have or have had prostate cancer. Check with your doctor or do some research on your own before you start taking it.

Flaxseed oil is one of the richest sources of omega 3 fatty acids available. If it is blended with cottage cheese, yoghurt or tofu, it is more easily absorbed by the body and acts like jumper leads, recharging your body's batteries.

Dr Budwig's proven three-step process for recharging your life battery is:

1. Take flaxseed oil, mixed with cottage cheese, tofu, etc.
2. Look at all food products that have a shelf life and if you see hydrogenated or partially hydrogenated fats in the ingredients list, put them back on the shelf, because they are carcinogenic.
3. Eat more vegetables and fruit (we all knew that anyway).

There are two more issues we need to know to make sensible decisions about eating to live well. The first is that to preserve and increase the shelf life (by stopping the oil going rancid) of many commercially available food products that contain polyunsaturated oil, the oil must be refined or treated. It is heated to high temperatures and becomes 'hydrogenated'. This hydrogenation not only saturates the oils, but also creates trans fatty acids which are known to be carcinogenic. Preservatives, also added, act as 'respiratory poisons' which basically suffocate the cells and stop the recharging of our life batteries.

These scientists suggest that we avoid eating foods with fats that have been treated to increase shelf life. And beware of foods with 'hidden saturated or treated fats' like cakes, biscuits, pastries, sausages and luncheon meats! Look very carefully at the lists of ingredients – if there are oils, you can be pretty certain that they are hydrogenated. (Margarine falls into this category, so if you thought you were being responsible and improving your health by eating margarine, a substantial body of research suggests 'stop using it now'!)

The second issue is that our body runs as one giant electro-chemical circuit. In other words, chemically generated electric currents make our hearts pump, our nerves send messages, our cells regenerate and reproduce, and our foods metabolise. So our bodies are electrically 'charged' and function something like cars. Like cars, we also have a 'car battery', a source of the power that drives us.

Highly unsaturated fats are full of electrons which are the things that can (very simply put) recharge our life batteries. Flaxseed oil when mixed with cottage cheese, yogurt or tofu releases lots of the electrons that make the fats very useful to individual cells in the daily renewal process of life. Hydrogenated fats have their electrons destroyed by the preserving process.

Electrons have a great attraction for oxygen and stimulate the 'breathing' of all our cells. These electrons are supposed to give us a feeling of wellbeing and 'lightness'.

Whether a cell thrives or dies appears to be determined by how fat and protein associate with it. Here's an interesting tidbit – the male sperm has over a thousand times more sulphurated protein (also in cottage cheese, tofu, etc.) than any other cell. The female ovum has bucket loads of highly unsaturated fats (like flax oil).

At the instant of fertilisation, the respiration of the cells increases a thousandfold. The cells start panting and breathing in loads of oxygen, and start reproducing at an amazing rate. I assume a similar effect occurs in normal cells when they are fed the flax/protein mixture – they regenerate and reproduce perfect cells (as long as the genetic code and a million other factors are OK!).

But wait – there's still more! Sunshine is a great source of electrons, and the oil/protein combo is the ideal mechanism for storing the sun's energy/electrons. So make sure you spend some time in the sun (with sunscreen, of course) to gather up all those little battery chargers!

Dr Budwig has convinced me. I've got my whole family on this regime and any of my friends who are still talking to me! If you can't bear the taste of the combination, mix it with a little pure honey (from a health-food shop) or some tamari or soy sauce. Hey, it's only one or two tablespoons a day, and it seems to affect every one of our cells, and if you read these scientists' more extensive scientific research, you'll be convinced as well! `

So, to be optimally well, to maximise our human physiological potential, from a nutrition viewpoint, one of the things we need to do is ingest essential fatty acids, blended with the protein I mentioned, eat more fruits and vegetables, and avoid supermarket items with long shelf lives. Do not cook with flax oil as the omega 3 is destroyed in the heating process. Happy recharging!

12

flax oil and life

In the previous article I have written about one of the most significant, yet simple, wellness findings I have come across. Flax oil (or flaxseed oil) is one of the richest sources of essential fatty acids (EFAs) – specifically omega 3.

EFAs are unbelievably important for healthy functioning of the body and in combating most of the diseases that affect us in our society today. Our bodies cannot manufacture all of them – we must eat foods that contain them. Not many foods we eat have the EFAs we need.

The one you are most likely to have heard about is omega 3 fatty acids. Remember when all the evidence was produced that heart disease is reduced by eating oily fish a few times a week or taking fish oil capsules? The magic ingredient in fish oil was (you guessed it!) the omega 3 fatty acids. Well, flax oil has three times more omega 3 fatty acids than fish oil.

In addition, EFAs are part of the building blocks of all the membranes of all the tissues in the body. That means without adequate levels of EFAs no cell in our body can function normally. Nor can it reproduce without mutating.

Long-term deficiency of EFAs has been associated with coronary disease, diabetes mellitis, breast and menstrual disorders, immune system problems, arthritis, skin disorders, inflammation, degenerative diseases, cancer, sterility in males and psychiatric disorders. Other than that, they're really not too important!

Other symptoms of omega 3 deficiencies are brittle finger-nails, increased need for sleep, carbohydrate cravings, excess gas, fatigue, brittle hair, grogginess on waking, irritability, inability to concentrate and headaches.

Pure unrefined flax oil must be produced under special conditions, then kept cool, in the dark and away from oxygen. Make sure the oil you buy is purchased direct from the manu-facturer or from a supplier who follows a stringent routine for transport and sale. Fresh oil has a mild, pleasant taste.

But wait – there's more! Coral Davies, the ever alert reader and producer of Stoney Creek Oil Products, grows flax and scours the world searching for new information about this life-giving (and life-restoring) substance. She sent me two articles and you need to know what's in them.

Firstly, chronic fatigue sufferers (post-viral fatigue syndrome), pay attention! A technical newsletter from Analytical Reference Laboratories reported a 1990 study from a Scandinavian medical journal. Sixty-three adults with post viral fatigue syndrome were involved in a heavy-duty, double-blind, and placebo-controlled (meaning scientifically valid!) research project. These people had been ill for one to seven years and suffered severe fatigue, muscle pains, dizziness, poor concentration and a variety of psychiatric symptoms.

All these people had their EFA levels tested and all were found to have very low levels, particularly in the red blood cells. These low levels were believed to be contributing (or dare I be more assertive than the study and say in part causing?) the symp-toms. After supplements of EFAs (by taking flax oil mixed with yoghurt, tofu, etc.), the EFA composition of their red blood cell phospholipids improved (meaning their red blood cells were much healthier).

Worldwide growing interest in EFAs and their importance led to an international convention on EFAs a few years ago. There is still a lot of confusion about the best combination of EFAs but the general flavour of all the research I have been able to source is that flax oil is the best (because it's the highest in omega 3 fatty acids) until we can grow hemp oil (marijuana) legally!

Anyway, the second hot piece of information you need comes from an American journal called *Total Health* which in 1993 outlined how the Food and Drug Administration (FDA) in America endorsed flax oil. Apparently the University of Toronto started studying flax oil and its benefits seven years ago, and results have shown that flax oil can lower serum cholesterol and prevent the growth of new cancer cells.

These results prompted the National Cancer Institute (NCI) to offer grants for more research into cancer and flax oil. At an experimental biology conference in 1993, the FDA and other researchers presented the following findings. Flaxseed/flax oil has the following possible effects:

- Certain levels of flax in the diet stimulated the immune system.
- Flax increased vitamin D levels and increased the retention of calcium, magnesium and phosphate.
- Ground flax seed had no negative effects on the liver or gut system and did not lower blood vitamin E levels.
- Flax is very high in lignans which have anti-tumour properties and may be linked to low incidence of breast and colon cancer.
- Flax is a good antioxidant.
- Ten per cent flax in the diet of rats could mimic the results of Tamoxifen, the mammary cancer-fighting drug, with no side effects.
- Adding eight per cent flax to the diet could help diabetic conditions caused by a high fat diet.
- Moderately high levels of flax were better at lowering triglycerides, total cholesterol and LDL (the 'bad' cholesterol) than the same level of oat bran.
- It can help with weight loss.

Udo Erasmus also suggests that the flax oil/protein combination (mentioned previously):

- is the best moisturiser for the skin and makes it supple and soft
- softens stools and eliminates constipation
- diminishes the effects of stress
- improves brain and nerve functioning and may improve school results.

So, that's it! If you want more energy and vitality, softer skin and stools, no more constipation, to feel less stressed, to protect yourself against cancer, to lessen your chance of becoming a diabetic, to reduce cholesterol, to stimulate your metabolism, to reduce your arthritic symptoms and to boost your immune system, to name a few benefits, then love that old flax oil/protein combination.

Although we don't know exactly how the body uses EFAs or exactly which are the best ones to take, the latest debate seems over whether flax oil or hemp oil is the best to take.

As hemp is illegal, my advice is to start with one tablespoon of flax oil per 45 kg body weight, blended with 3 tablespoons of cottage cheese, skim milk powder, or yoghurt or tofu. (If one tablespoon is too much for you and makes you feel unwell, start with smaller quantities. You may also choose to have a doctor check your EFA levels first.) Add two tablespoons of flax meal for fibre, phytooestrogens and lignans, except if you have coeliac disease.

Take some evening primrose oil as well, until they work out a way to legalise hemp!

Also by Amanda Gore

Log on to **www.amandagore.com**
to find out more about Amanda Gore's seminars, books, videos
and audio programmes, or to subscribe to her FREE monthly
email newsletter.

Or, for further information, call:

Julianna Millar in Australia (02 6298 3144)
Somer McCormick in the USA (214 752 4640)

TRAINING TOOLS, SCHOOLS, BUSINESS, PERSONAL GIFTS

If you are a training manager, Amanda's videos are ideal tools.
Many of Australia's largest organisations use them as part of their
induction training programs.

School libraries use a range of her books and videos. If yours
doesn't have a look at the website to see what is available.

And Amanda's books and videos make terrific presents that
have value for life! If you have friends or family who are in need
of an emotional lift, are going through exams or need to lighten
up – consider a gift that they will thank you for.

FAMILIES

Many people have told us that they show Amanda's *Stress Busters* (*Live Out Loud*) video at family get-togethers, to great effect! At the end, people are laughing and connected, and have a new 'language' for overcoming the usual family difficulties.

Some others have shown the *Brain Sex* videos at dinner parties, with hysterical results!

VIDEOS

Stress Busters (*Live Out Loud* in the US) – A video on leading and living to the max! Funny, interactive and useful as a training tool in your organisation. Full of practical information and tips to enhance your communication, business and personal relationships. It's all about busting stress, increasing energy and enjoying life more!

Brain Sex – A humorous look at the differences in the way men and women communicate and how to bridge the chasm. It might make you laugh – but it's useful as well!

KITS/COMBOS

Different kits are available depending on which hemisphere you are in. Log on to the website or phone the numbers given for further information.

BOOKS

The Office Athlete – A guide to staying well at work. In her past, Amanda was a physiotherapist and ergonomics consultant. This is a compilation of her ideas and strategies for maintaining pain-free office spaces, and for setting up children's work areas to avoid the neck and back aches that so often accompany long hours of study or computer use.

Stress Busters – You will begin busting stress from the very first page. Ideal for those who are too stressed to read much!

AUDIO PROGRAMMES

What's the Difference that Makes the Difference? – A set of six one-hour audio tapes, covering how to communicate more effectively, sell more, bust stress, feel better and generally have more fun in life!

Live out Loud – After many requests for reminders of Amanda's techniques, we've put the soundtrack of *Live Out Loud* onto a CD. Now Amanda can accompany you in your car or at home.